Ending Unnecessary Suffering

"Peter Ralston has created a mighty tome that clearly lays out why we suffer, the mechanics behind our suffering, and solutions that we can actually use to end our personal suffering. The practices offered bring us to awareness, and that is a beautiful doorway to freedom from pain and freedom from suffering. In a day and age when we can experience many difficulties just by living life, *Ending Unnecessary Suffering* is a gift to us all."

SELINA MAITREYA, SPIRITUAL TEACHER AND AUTHOR OF
RAISE YOUR FREQUENCY, TRANSFORM YOUR LIFE

"Ralston has clearly outlined the cause of unnecessary suffering, which is the distinction between concept and experience. Concept separates us from experience, and this separation, he explains, is a major cause of suffering that is internally created. Experience is in the here and now and is closer to a state of being that doesn't add to the limitations of concept that leads to suffering. He offers practices to move from understanding to a functional state of experience. There is much in this book to help you become a person who lives from experience if you follow the process he presents."

ROBERT NADEAU, AIKIDO 8TH DAN SHIHAN

Ending Unnecessary Suffering

How to Create a Powerful, Complete, and Peaceful Life

A Sacred Planet Book

PETER RALSTON

Park Street Press
Rochester, Vermont

Park Street Press
One Park Street
Rochester, Vermont 05767
www.ParkStPress.com

Park Street Press is a division of Inner Traditions International

Sacred Planet Books are curated by Richard Grossinger, Inner Traditions editorial board member and cofounder and former publisher of North Atlantic Books. The Sacred Planet collection, published under the umbrella of the Inner Traditions family of imprints, includes works on the themes of consciousness, cosmology, alternative medicine, dreams, climate, permaculture, alchemy, shamanic studies, oracles, astrology, crystals, hyperobjects, locutions, and subtle bodies.

Cataloging-in-Publication Data for this title is available from the Library of Congress

ISBN 979-8-88850-118-4 (print)
ISBN 979-8-88850-119-1 (ebook)

Printed and bound in the United States by Lake Book Manufacturing, LLC

10 9 8 7 6 5 4 3 2 1

Text design and layout by Virginia Scott Bowman
This book was typeset in Garamond Premier Pro and Futura with Begum, Forma DJR Micro, and Span used as display typefaces

To send correspondence to the author of this book, mail a first-class letter to the author c/o Inner Traditions • Bear & Company, One Park Street, Rochester, VT 05767, and we will forward the communication, or contact the author directly at **PeterRalston.com**.

Contents

PART III
Investigating Our Experience

Stop Putting Your Hand in Boiling Water

IT'S NOT NEWS TO ANY OF US THAT our experience often includes various forms of suffering. From time to time we suffer physical pain. Yet, for most of us, mental and emotional suffering actually dominates our lives far more than the simple pain of stubbing a toe. Unknown to pretty much everyone, however, is that this domain of suffering is unnecessary.

This form of unnecessary suffering is pretty much unique to humans. We worry, long for, fear, despair, desire, feel less than, are dissatisfied, get depressed, feel flawed, and on and on. Ever experienced any of this domain of distress? These and many more are based solely on concepts—on figments of mind. It seems like they are just necessary aspects of life. But they aren't.

This may seem far-fetched because we live inside of this conceptual reality as if it is an absolute truth. But it's not. To get a better handle on how much suffering we create solely through conceptualizing, notice rabbits don't experience this form of suffering. They have no idea that there could be more to life, or that it's possible to have any other experience than what they're having. Notice they don't suffer much of what we suffer. Because of our automatic and natural arrogance that humans are so much better than all the "lower" creatures, we overlook a significant flaw in the makeup of our own experience.

These simpler creatures don't worry or fret like we do or fear the future or crave anything not available. They don't imagine that they are somehow flawed or less than they should be. Have you ever seen a three-legged dog? They don't seem to have any disturbance at all because of it. Notice, or imagine, the difference between their experience and yours, and the degree of suffering they don't seem to have, simply because they don't have the complex conceptual "ability" that for us tends to run amok.

Consider this contrast. Probably from time to time you have come close to a simple and present experience of simply *being* in this moment. I suspect you enjoyed that experience. So why devote so much time and effort to the plethora of activities that create so much unnecessary suffering? Obviously because it doesn't seem to be in your hands. But this book changes all that and helps put you in the driver's seat. In order to do that, however, you'll need to understand how your mind works so you can free yourself from the automatic programming and habits that create this suffering.

For this communication to make a difference you need to experience that all these forms of distress are something you are *doing* and not imposed upon you against your will. This perspective is not the norm. Almost everyone thinks suffering is imposed upon them and not something they're generating. But once you experience what's true in this matter, you can stop doing what causes suffering and it won't occur. Sound too good to be true?

It is possible to eliminate most of what we suffer. The reason we don't is twofold. One reason is ignorance. Almost no one has been introduced to this possibility, nor do we grasp how our own minds create our suffering. Another reason, beyond our ignorance: we have automatic drives we take for granted that press us into mental-emotional activities that cause suffering, but we don't connect the dots.

I sometimes use an analogy that may not be the best, but it makes the point. Through an impulse created by our greed, if we reach for a diamond resting on the bottom of a bucket of boiling water, we will experience a lot of pain. But as long as we don't connect the pain with our actions we will continue to stick our hand into boiling water. This might seem a bit obscure, but the point is we are actually doing stuff that creates our suffering. We don't have to do it, but not doing it requires that we become aware of *what* we are doing and *that* we are doing it. It isn't at all impossible, but it does require seriously challenging overlooked assumptions and ignorance.

At this point, you might wonder what makes me qualified to speak on this subject? How is it that I can assert such things with a straight face? Perhaps you regard my blabbing as simply my opinion. But that really isn't the case. Some contributions to my "expertise" might come from having spent decades mastering the fighting arts—beyond all traditions—allowing me to become the first non-Asian to win the full-contact World Championships in China. But how does that relate to understanding the causes of suffering?

My approach to mastering such interactive skills was the same as my approach to increasing consciousness. I studied the body from the ground up and increased the sensitivity of my nervous system. As well, I studied the mind for many decades and discovered the dynamics and principles involved in effective interaction. I broke it all down and learned directly what's going on in both mind and body. From these efforts, I developed a high level of sensitivity and mind control and discovered a great deal about how the mind works, how it gets us into trouble, and how to overcome that tendency.

Commensurate with such studies, however, the major contributor to understanding suffering came from decades of studying the human condition and becoming conscious of the nature of self and our perceived reality. Through a lot of contemplation, I had what Zen people call enlightenment experiences. This is actually where my real authority in these matters comes from.

I'm not saying that enlightenment directly provided all this knowledge about suffering. What it did provide, however, is an ability to step outside of the taken-for-granted world in which we live, thus providing a clear contrast to better discern the activities of mind that do cause suffering. This discovery took a lot of hard work and investigation, but having some "nothing from which to come" made it possible. Anyway, that's a short version of why I might have something to offer outside the norm.

There is much to become conscious of, much that can be done, and much that can be created in the life you live. It takes some study, and this study can't be comprised of just simplistic steps taken to give easy access to some miracle cure. You must become conscious of what is actually occurring in your own experience and learn to control the workings of your mind. It isn't all that difficult, but it has to be real, and for it to be real you will need to really grasp what is being communicated.

Some of what will be put forward requires serious investigation on your part, even if sometimes it seems a bit abstract. The first section of this book isn't actually necessary to begin your work on suffering. So if you find these chapters too difficult or if they seem unrelated to your experience, you are welcome to bypass them and go right to part 2.

Our suffering, however, is only one aspect of the reality in which we live. Without grasping this reality as a whole, we won't truly grasp or effectively relate to the suffering we want to avoid. If some aspect of this investigation is not your cup of tea, however, you can ignore it if you like and look for more useful stuff. But be warned, the usefulness of what interests you will be less powerful without understanding the whole truth about the reality in which it exists.

The ability to step outside of your experiences and see them for what they are provides a new way to relate to them. This includes ending suffering, which I suspect will be everyone's favorite subject. Yet in order to end suffering you have to really grasp what's going on. I will lay it out as best I can, and I promise it is really possible and available, but you have to do the work. Beyond the subject of suffering, the last sections of the book provide many generally unknown possibilities that can empower you in your ability to create a more powerful and effective life.

Every book I have written has had the same purpose—to transform the experience of the reader in some way. It is not to convince them of some belief system, or to pass on some intellectual knowledge, or to entertain. It is to increase the consciousness of the reader about the subject matter and change their experience because of it—either learning more about the nature of what they already experience or becoming conscious of stuff that they never knew existed. That's my job. Assuming I've done my job, that's what will happen. Given I've done my job, however, increasing consciousness and changing your experience is up to you.

PART I

❧

Foundations of Our Experience

Part 1 is offered in an attempt to assist you in breaking free of many taken-for-granted assumptions hidden within your experience. This is done to lay a foundation, preparing you to better tackle the subject of suffering. That's why I start by delving into matters that at first may not seem to be related to improving your life. Yet understanding and creating some freedom from what binds you to your dominant and overwhelming self-experience allows you to more effectively tackle what does make a difference.

In order to get the most from this material, I will pull excerpts from some of my other books. Sorry if you find yourself suddenly dumped into the deep end of the pool with material that may be a bit out of context. Again, if you find the depth of this work too difficult you are welcome to bypass it and go right to the second part and begin the work on ending suffering. But if, after you finish with that study, you find you still can't control your mind and detach from deeply held source concepts, you can always come back and go over part 1 to see if it helps increase your understanding and mental abilities.

◇ Excerpts from Support Material ◇

Excerpts from *The Book of Not Knowing: Exploring the True Nature of Self, Mind, and Consciousness* (North Atlantic Books, 2010) and *Whereof One Cannot Speak* (unpublished) are given distinct design treatments in this book for ease of use. You will find the excerpts from *The Book of Not Knowing* framed with the paragraphs numbered as in the original, allowing you to easily continue your studies in this earlier book should you wish. Excerpts from my as yet unpublished *Whereof One Cannot Speak*, which consists of deeper support material, are set against a shaded background.

CHAPTER ONE

Concept versus Experience

WE BEGIN OUR STUDY OF SUFFERING by understanding that concept is very different from experience. Concept is a function of and exists solely within the mind. An idea is not the same as an object. In order for us to tackle the causes of suffering it is essential to know the difference between everything we do that is conceptual in nature and what is not.

We already make a distinction between mind and objects. Yet because we relate to even the biological and objective world via concept, a great deal of concept is confused with what exists in an objective sense. Although the difference between concept and experience might seem clear on its face, when we look into it we find there is a great deal of conflation and confusion between the two. So our first job is to become clear as to what is concept and what is experience.

To start us off, let's take some excerpts from *The Book of Not Knowing* on these subjects—if you've already read these, keep in mind they bear repeating. Beyond refreshing your experience, set out to get it more deeply and as an active part of everything of which you are aware. If there are consequences for confusing concept for experience, we need to better know what concept is and isn't.

WHAT IS A CONCEPT?

6:14 But what actually is a concept? There is some confusion about what is meant by concept, so let's look into it by starting with a definition or two:

Concept

1. A general idea derived or inferred from specific instances or occurrences.
2. Something formed in the mind; a thought or notion.
3. A scheme; a plan.

Conceptual

1. Of, pertaining to, or relating to mental conceptions.

6:15 We often think of a concept as a general idea, or a vaguely organized mental image: *I've never been to a barn raising, but I get the concept.* But anything that is fabricated in the mind is conceptual. A concept is unreal in the objective sense, meaning nothing substantial exists. Some people might call it a "conceptual object" since it appears to us as some "thing," but a concept has no mass, no location, occupies no space—it exists solely within our mental perceptions or imagination. This does not make it any less powerful, simply less objective. What we need to grasp at this juncture is that concept is not something that exists of its own accord, but is the summation of a mental process. It *refers* to something; it is never the thing itself.

6:16 Concepts are ways of knowing, and everything we know is conceptual. Some examples of concepts are interpretation, memory, beliefs, ideas, notions, dreams, imagination, thoughts, fantasies, visualizations, assumptions, and anything else that is a product of the mind. We could even say that emotions are conceptual in nature since they are produced through conceptualization. Concepts are not limited to one aspect of mental activity; they comprise the entire field of mind and as such they influence almost everything of which we are aware.

6:17   Abstractions, such as a mathematical formula, a daydream, or a decorating idea, are easily recognized as concepts because they are different from our normal experience and perceptions. But one of the main jobs of concept is to mimic our everyday perceptions and experiences. This means that a perception such as the sight of a bus can be somehow "known" when there is no bus around. We can "see" the bus in our minds, so to speak. It is the same with sounds—like remembering a song—as well as smells, tastes, and touch. Anything we've perceived, and even things we haven't, can be conceptually perceived in the mind. Whenever we remember something, we are "reperceiving" past events. Given we are conscious that these events have passed, we know them as memories, but they are conceptual nonetheless. Concept not only *mimics* reality, however, it serves to help *create* reality.

6:18   When we look at a tree, we imagine that we are merely perceiving the tree when in actuality we are interpreting or "knowing" it as a tree. We may see some object there, but when we interpret it as a tree something more is now perceived that wasn't there previously. This is a conceptual superimposition placed upon what is perceived, without which we would not see a "tree." We don't recognize that we live entirely within a conceptual reality any more than a fish recognizes that water has always surrounded him.

> 6:19 Everything we perceive, whether it's an object or mental image, is subject to interpretation—making sense of incoming data so we can recognize and categorize it. Interpretation allows us to order our world, which requires mental processes that are all conceptual. It is also true that much of what is "experienced" as oneself is really a concept rather than an experience. And as I've suggested already, there is a distinction we need to make between the *experience* of being and the *concept* of self.

Exercise for Identifying Concepts

Bring to mind all of the concepts you've been involved with throughout your life. Keep digging into it for a while. Notice it is a huge amount of concepts! Now take a look into your current experience and notice every concept you can find that is influencing your experience right now. Keep your attention on the difference between concept and experience. Then, when you put this book down at some point, spend some time noticing all the concepts you have throughout a period of time. Remember, you have to do the work—otherwise, ending suffering won't occur.

Now I'm going to say several things briefly and quickly, but they are important to grasp. Don't overlook these important points because of their brevity; they are central to our work on suffering. Grasping these realities begins to change our relationship to life and experience, but this is just an introduction—a small crash course in the existential nature of concept and life. Take it seriously and consider the reality that is being asserted, even if you don't see the practicality of it or how it relates to suffering quite yet.

Realize that concept is not real in the sense that it is not objective; it is occurring as a figment or activity of mind. Since it is solely a figment of mind it can be false—meaning whatever the concept is about may not be true or representing reality accurately. And, strange as it may seem, it is never what is actually being experienced as the present moment of life. Clearly, concept influences what you experience, but I want you to get that it is not what you experience except through this influence.

It's not what we think but what we *experience* that is where real life occurs. Life only occurs now in this present moment . . . and will always only occur now in this present moment. This objective and occurring activity is what I'm calling "real life." Concept creates the idea of a future and a past but these are not occurring as real life, except as ideas. Concept also creates judgments, comparisons, and many other relations to what is perceived, but this is still not what is perceived. Objective life is only occurring within what is perceived as what's occurring in this moment and only this moment.

I invite you to notice that it is *always* now. It never stops being now and everything that occurs, occurs now. Can you get that? It might seem like life occurs in the past and the future, but those are only concepts that occur now.

What's also true is that memory is not an accurate representation of what actually occurred, and imagination cannot be a representation of what will occur because it hasn't happened. A guess is not a fact. What's more, your conceptual-activities are almost always seriously distorted about what is, was, or will be. You should know this, but it isn't necessary in order to understand that concept isn't experience and real life takes place only in experience. So let's take a look at experience. Again, from *The Book of Not Knowing*:

WHAT IS AN EXPERIENCE?

4:18 Take a moment and notice your experience right now. What does it consist of? The physical pressure of sitting, the temperature of the room, looking around, your mood and attitudes—whatever is so for you right now. Maybe you're flattered by the attentions of a cat purring on your lap, or maybe the neighbor's mowing is a background irritation. Perhaps you're still smarting from an argument with your mate, or you might be bored with what you're reading. All that you're aware of right now is your present experience.

4:19   Experience is always taking place right here and now, and it's always the only thing we've got going on. But what is it? It's surprisingly difficult to address the real nature of our own experience. There's a lot in the way of discerning this nature, and what is in the way is difficult to see. As is often useful in making new distinctions, we'll begin by looking into what we hold as "the obvious."

Some basic definitions of the word *experience:*

1. The apprehension of what's occurring through the senses.
2. To personally undergo.

4:20   Within our awareness, we experience or perceive many things on many levels at once. We see a telephone in the room, but we also wonder if Jill is going to call. We are aware of both of these perceptions, and, although it's usually overlooked, we can notice the difference between perceiving an object (the phone) and perceiving a thought that someone might call. When the phone actually rings we experience an activity, full of sensation and sound. Simply imagining the call, however, we have to say there exists no activity except in our own thinking.

4:21   Yet even when we experience an actual phone call, many concepts fill much of the space in that experience. We may react to something, such as being surprised at what the caller says. This reaction isn't the same as the information received, nor is it the sound we're hearing. The feeling of surprise is a separate mental-emotional activity. Is this an experience of the phone call? Ordinarily, we would say yes, we experienced a surprising phone call. We combine our reaction with the activity of hearing what's said, and we lump it all together as the "experience." Normally this just doesn't matter to us, but it's useful to recognize that there are a few things going on.

4:22   Notice that the perception of our reaction is different in "kind" from the perception of an activity or an object. Generally, we experience a thought just as we experience, for example, a rock. What we refer to with the word *experience* usually means "to perceive"—we perceive thoughts and emotions arising, and we perceive objects and movement. But I want to propose a new possibility here that suggests we can *experience* the thought versus just thinking it, or *experience* the rock versus just seeing it. The difference between perceiving something and experiencing it can perhaps be found within our level of participation in the encounter.

4:23   When we experience something, we "personally undergo" an encounter with it. The difference between a thought and an object is pretty easy to see. A rock is clearly outside of our imagination. It seems not of our own making and provides consistent information that we seem to have no choice but to receive. The rock is hard every time it hits us in the head, and we can see its shape and color, which also tend to remain consistent. We perceive these things as independent of our imagination. We say we experience the rock when we are clear there is a rock present and we perceive it or personally undergo an encounter with it. It's not difficult for us to discern the difference between concepts, such as our fascination with the rock or our anger at the rock, and the rock itself. When we do that, and put our awareness on the rock independent of any notions or reactions about it, then we are "experiencing" the rock. But what about experiencing a concept, like an idea or belief?

4:24   We do seem to "personally undergo" our thoughts and feelings, which is why we often state that we're experiencing them. Our emotions, ideas, impressions, and memories enter our awareness in much the same way as anything we see and hear. So how do we distinguish between experiencing an idea and just having an idea? Beyond the presence of the idea as a mere figment of our imagination—like all ideas—how would we "experience" something that is itself a concept?

4:25   Adhering to a specific definition of the word *experience* provides us with some solid ground on which to begin sorting this out. If we define experience as "whatever we personally encounter as real and not merely imagined," an idea becomes an experience for us when we have an immediate, personal encounter with the reality of the idea itself or what the idea represents. We're not having a thought about the idea, nor are we merely choosing to believe in it.

It is simply a conceptual-activity occurring now, but the subject of the idea is still just an imagination. As with the rock, first we need to get the idea as itself—as conceptual-activity—and not anything else.

An object is only perceived not generated. On the other hand, a concept is generated in order for it to be perceived. The difference between having a concept versus experiencing the concept is this: in order to experience it we must get it as an activity we are doing, in present time, as opposed to imagining it to be a reality we are perceiving. If the concept comes to us as if it is a reality we merely perceive, then we are simply having the thought. On the other hand, if we get we are doing it, and get what we are doing, we can experience the doing and so experience the activity that is a concept. Do you get the difference between "having" an idea and "experiencing" the activity that is the idea?

As I elaborated in *The Book of Not Knowing* (4:27), "on the one hand we have an experience of some matter, and on the other hand we have thoughts *about* the matter. Whenever we confuse our knowledge, associations, beliefs, and fantasies with something we encounter— whether it's a rock or an idea—we're not having an experience of what's actually there. We're having our thoughts and beliefs about it, and this is in a completely different domain from experience." In this work, we will need to experience what's true about the experience of living life, not add more thoughts and fantasies about it. Are you clear about the difference between experience and concept?

Again, experience only occurs now. Anything not experienced in this moment is not experienced. If some supposed "experience" is not happening now, then by definition it is a concept not an experience. People often don't get this because when we have experienced something we remember it as an experience, but currently it isn't. If we aren't experiencing it now, what we have is a concept of what was experienced.

Experience always degrades into concept. The moment a perceived experience has passed it is no longer an experience. In the very next moment, anything remaining about that experience is a concept. We live as if these are the same thing, but they really aren't. It is essential that we get this.

Life, as an occurring event, is occurring only in this moment. Take a look. This experience you are having now is your experience of life; everything else is a concept. And very likely whatever you're experiencing now is also inundated with tons of concepts influencing this experience. Get that this is always true. The main thing to get now is that concept isn't experience and real life only exists in experience. Can you get that?

INCORPORATING AN ASSERTION

Before going on, it may be useful to look a bit more into your job in this study. With each point made, the first thing you need to do is understand it. If you don't understand what's being asserted, you can't proceed effectively. This means you have to get beyond personal preferences and beliefs and truly listen to the assertion as it is communicated, not as you want it to be. You also have to set out to *experience* the assertion not just hear about it. Sometimes this can be a challenge and take some work.

Once you understand intellectually, next you need to validate the assertion in your experience. Find examples of it in your past, your life, or your current experience. Once you validate it with a sampling, proving to yourself it's reality, you need to go further. Most people stop here, thinking that once their minds have proven the assertion is real, their job is over. But it isn't.

After validating the assertion by getting a hit on it here and there, you need to move to the more important stage of realizing it as a continuous activity within your current and ongoing experience. Not just intellectually knowing the dynamic is true but grasping it as constantly occurring and dominating your experience to whatever degree it does. This is an important ingredient for developing a real and effective relationship to the work of ending suffering.

Intellectual knowledge or even proof of validity through sampling isn't enough to change your experience. It might change your knowledge base, but not your experience. And in order to end suffering you need to change your experience. You can't do that unless you get these assertions as real and occurring.

Once you get that far, if the dynamic is dysfunctional you need to transcend it or change it. To do that, you must get it's something you're doing and are responsible for. If the assertion itself isn't dysfunctional—but is simply true or what's going on (as is much of what's addressed in this section)—you still need to be able to understand the dynamics involved. Now, apply this to what you've read so far and all that you are about to read.

HOW DOES CONCEPT DOMINATE YOUR EXPERIENCE?

In this work, it is essential that you grasp the real nature of concept and the many ways it's fused with your experience of yourself, life, and reality. We will tackle this in several ways throughout the book. Again, from *The Book of Not Knowing*:

> 6:3   Even at an early age, human children have an astounding capacity for creating concepts and a natural ability to make up entire "worlds" in which to be and act. We think of it as merely playing, but make-believe is more than just an imaginative way for children to amuse themselves. What such activities really do is train their ability to conceptualize.
>
> 6:4   The phrase *make-believe* correctly suggests that a belief is "made." As children, we spend countless hours constructing fictitious roles, storylines, and circumstances, inventing the necessary sets, props, and partners to act them out. All these are created as a "reality" so that we can act in accord with the pretense. As with kittens, the motivation to play appears to be simply that it's fun, but without such skills

we could not function as intelligent creatures capable of perceiving a great deal more than what is in front of us.

6:5   Of course, interwoven with any child's play is a constant learning process in which, piece by piece, certain observations and beliefs are made real. Some of these serve the practical purpose of survival—"hot" or "sharp" objects are not to be touched, and it's dangerous to play in the street or talk to strangers. Also, from a very early age, children pick up subtle instruction in views and values. They might learn that knowledge, talent, or possessions are evidence of a "deserving" person (and the lack of these indicates an "unworthy" person), that the beliefs of the family and community are correct while all other beliefs are incorrect.

6:6   Being predisposed to internalize these lessons, children often reinforce them in their play. They enjoy escaping from imaginary dangers, caring for stuffed animals or dolls, imitating figures who seem powerful to them like a queen or superhero, or acting as if a pretend fire is hot. They invent roles and situations in which they can demonstrate the personal qualities, skills, and knowledge that are admired in their family and community. Make-believe can be a lot like making real.

6:7   It's not difficult to think of a child's imaginative play as a conceptual-activity, but we don't usually consider that everything we perceive as adults is subject to a similar if more sophisticated system of conceptualization. In fact, one difference between adult and child is that the child is more likely to recognize that he's the author of his fantasies. He might get annoyed when his world of make-believe is interrupted, not wanting to admit that he isn't really

Superman, or that his magical energy beams may indeed not be all powerful, but when Mom calls him to dinner he knows it's time to return to the "real" world. As adults we are far less likely to do so. By the time we reach adulthood, much of what we "know" actually falls into the category of "make-believe" but we don't recognize it as such. Having thought this way for as long as we can remember, we take it for granted that our beliefs are real.

Unlike a child, as an adult we are not becoming a self, we already are one. This requires a different relationship to make-believe, but as an adult we rarely notice that so much of our experienced reality is made up. For example, one of the key elements that we don't recognize as make-believe is living in relation to ideals. Holding ideals as important images we should attain is a mistake, and yet they dominate much of our background sense of life. A child can believe in Santa Claus but an adult should not. Yet adults believe in so much that is really no more real or attainable than Santa Claus.

6:9   When we start considering all that we have adopted and made into our reality and view, we begin to discover a great deal that is seen as "reality" when it really isn't. We have beliefs that we recognize as beliefs—I believe in God, or I believe in the tooth fairy—and yet we have many more beliefs that we just assume rather than recognize. We hold many notions that are taken for granted as a part of life or reality. We may assume that children are innocent, humankind is becoming more advanced, thinking is what "I" do that I call thinking, emotions are what we suppose they are and are necessary aspects of being human, love is universal, disease can be cured, all "good" religions are based on valid truths, contrary belief systems are ignorant at best, animals have emotions, something written in a book is likely true, my self is unique and meaningful, not to know is bad. These and countless other "truths" like them are only beliefs, but still we may live as if they are correct.

6:10   So many ideas have been instilled in us for so long that it can be a challenge just to recognize our beliefs, much less disengage from them. This is not necessarily an easy thing to grasp, even when you want to. You might take on faith or figure out intellectually that a great deal of your perceived world is purely conceptual, but that does very little to provide you with the means to challenge or transcend it. You need to have experience after experience, and insight after insight that this is actually the case. You need to do the work of recognizing the true nature of your own perceptions. Even if you've made such observations in the past, the work isn't done until it's done.

SUGGESTIONS FOR CONTEMPLATION
Recognizing Your Beliefs

Take a moment and look into your own mind. What do you believe? Try to bring to mind everything you believe is true but haven't personally experienced. Identify all of your beliefs, and any belief systems you might embrace and what they are all about.

Whatever comes to mind with such questions is something you can begin to investigate. The beliefs themselves are not so important—what we're mostly looking at now is how you hold them as true.

Can you uncover some assumptions that you live with but don't notice they're only an assumed frame of mind? For instance, what do you believe about your life? Is it an exciting adventure or a woeful sentence to be served until death? What do you think is true about life in general?

Notice that no matter what you come up with, it's conceptual. It's an idea within a web of ideas that helps make up your sense of life and reality.

Next, think about your relationship with different family members, your family's values, and what you think and feel about your family—whatever comes up, just notice any ideas and beliefs you have regarding your family.

Now, do the same thing with your country. What arises when you think about your country? What comes up when you think about various other countries?

Now do the same for yourself. What do you believe is true about you? Who are you? Are you sure? Can you uncover every judgment and assumption about yourself? What comes to mind when you think about yourself?

Notice there are a multitude of taken-for-granted ideas, feelings, associations, and judgments that constitute a perception of yourself. Grasp that every one of these is conceptual.

Every modern individual has a very complex and multilayered conceptual matrix that comprises the simple perception called "self." It is very useful to be in touch with what that is for you. Notice you run into a conceptual sense of yourself everywhere you turn because your experience is actually dominated by concepts and beliefs.

Notice that with each of these subjects there are a multitude of taken-for-granted ideas, feelings, associations, and judgments that constitute a perception of that whole matter for you. Take a moment and see if you can pick out what you actually feel and think about yourself, your life, your family, and your culture and country.

Regardless of the specifics that came up, the amount of thoughts and feelings is quite significant, isn't it? And it's all conceptual. Do you begin to see how many concepts are fused with your experience?

These suggestions are based on "Exercises in Recognizing Your Beliefs" (6:11–6:13) in *The Book of Not Knowing*.

INTERPRETATION AND MEANING

Even our perceptions that for all the world seem to be presently occurring still have very significant conceptual influence and dominance. Back to *The Book of Not Knowing*:

6:20   In simple terms, every perception we have is understood in relation to the concepts we have about what is being perceived. Once we learn to glimpse perception *prior to* our conceptual additions, we begin to understand the nature of concept and how it can limit us in our ability to experience. I'm not suggesting that we attempt to live without concept completely, but that we need to be aware of how concept dominates our perceptions and experience. We've already touched on this notion, but now let's look into it in more detail and depth.

6:21   Pure perception is incomprehensible to us. What we commonly call perception is really the interpretation of a meaningless phenomenon into a specific and useful "cognition." Fundamentally, a perception is simply a sensory encounter with some object or occurrence, and is without association or emotional charge.

6:22   There are two major conceptual contributors that dominate all of our experience: "interpretation" and "meaning." Since perception as itself is meaningless, what we perceive is useless without interpretation. The mere fact of seeing an object, hearing a sound, or feeling a sensation means nothing unless we know what it *is* and how it relates to *us*. To make sense of what we perceive, we automatically associate, classify, and interpret the meaningless data that is available. First, everything perceived is quickly interpreted so as to determine what it is—a flower, a squeak, a dog, a chair, soft, fast, a feeling, a person. Having conceptually identified what something is, we then immediately relate it to ourselves.

6:23 No matter what we perceive, once we interpret it in some basic way, we will go on to assess its value or threat to us by associating it with an array of past experiences and beliefs, and so supply it with meaning. This meaning renders the thing ugly, expensive, mine, hers, sacred, too big, useful, ridiculous, friendly, dangerous, or what have you. Once meaning is attached, our minds will immediately infuse the thing with some "emotional" charge, subtle or gross, to indicate in a feeling-sense how we should relate to it. This charge is based on the value or threat that a thing or notion has relative to us, and so this feeling-reaction contains information suggesting particular behavior— should we run or feed it a biscuit? Such feeling-charge manifests as attraction, fear, disinterest, annoyance, desire, boredom, importance, repulsion, and so on, as well as many such feelings far too subtle to warrant a name. The application of interpretation, meaning, and emotional charge occurs so fast and automatically that we do not distinguish any of these as separate activities within our whole experience.

6:24 This mechanism is a remarkable feature of the human mind—a rapid means of converting all perceptions into a self-relating form which enables us to take the necessary actions to insure our safety and survival. It's wise to remember, however, that everything we think we "know" is an interpretation. Every bit of information we take in is influenced and altered by our particular set of beliefs, assumptions, and associations. These alterations are conceptual "add-ons" that strongly influence our experience of whatever is perceived. What we react to is not the object itself but rather the interpretation and meaning that we ourselves apply to the object.

6:25   The process that we apply to objects of perception also works the same way on our own thoughts, emotions, and sensations. We associate them with the past, we assess their meaning and value—just about any reaction we can have to physical objects will also arise in relation to our own mental processes. Our ideas and beliefs and, in a way, our entire history are applied to everything that comes into our awareness—whether it's people and objects or our own thoughts and feelings.

6:26   What we know as reality is influenced by the concepts with which we interpret it. From "tree" to "hot" to "disgusting," what something means to us predetermines how we will perceive it. Yet this relationship between concept and reality is so seamless it is undetectable. The car "is" beautiful in our eyes, the apple "is" delightful in our mouths. Our reactions to an ugly and dangerous monster are pretty much the same thing to us as the experience of the monster itself.

6:27   Unless we make the distinction between our additions and what's there, we can't become conscious of what's actually there. Our whole experience of self and life is conceptually dominated. This means that we are not simply experiencing life and who we are; we're also constantly "imagining" life and who we are. Since it doesn't seem like it's our imagination we're perceiving, we don't know the difference between what we are adding and what is there.

Can you recognize that this conceptual influence acts on your personal experience in this way? It is within the conceptual domain that our suffering is generated. So as we proceed, we will need to discover which conceptual-activities actually generate our suffering. Better understanding the whole domain of concept in every form is our first task toward doing so.

There is nothing either good or bad,
but thinking makes it so.

WILLIAM SHAKESPEARE

CONCEPTS HELD AS IF THEY ARE OBJECTIVE REALITY

When something is held to be true or real—existing outside of our imagination—we hold it in a different category than something that's known to be just a concept. In the hierarchy of perceptions, we relegate abstract ideas to a lower rung of importance than objective reality. We may not like what the bus driver thinks about us, but we'll be sure to get out of the way of the bus.

Experience tells us we need to take that solid objectivity seriously. Even if we had the belief or fantasy that we could fly, when the bus bears down and flying isn't an option, we will jump aside instead. We respect the uncompromising aspects of objective reality, yet often blur the line of distinction between it and our mental activities. In so doing, each of us frequently perceives an idea as if it were a self-evident truth.

For example, someone might imagine that sex is somehow evil, or that his political party embodies the only correct view of human relations, or that her religion defines the nature of reality, or that some belief system has the only real description of the universe, or any number of notions, many of which are far too subtle or ingrained to easily recognize. But all of these are simply concepts that are believed to be representative of what's objectively true. And they aren't.

We stand just as firmly on many assumptions about ourselves. When someone says that he is worthless, we may know clearly that he is not, but for him, this self-description is a fact of his existence. The assumptions surrounding this "truth" are so ingrained in him that he can't see it as merely a powerful concept that influences his every thought and action. This trap makes what is only imagined in our minds seem like something objectively so.

Such a distinction is significant because what we can and can't do in relation to objects is different from what we can and can't do in relation to concepts. For example, if you have no legs, there is little you can do to change that. Pretending you have legs doesn't improve your running skills. If you think you are bad or stupid, clumsy or worthless, and that these assessments exist in the same category as having no legs, then you are just as stuck with them as you would be with a wheelchair. Although they are only assumptions that you've adopted or been trained to believe, they are deeply programmed and are perceived as if they are permanent traits. On the other hand, if you truly realize that these attributes are conceptual in nature, immediately you will experience the possibility that you can change them or get free of them altogether.

Shifting your self-concept in some way does indeed change your perception of yourself—but if this is something you desire, it's ineffective to rush ahead without a proper foundation. Such a change is rarely easy because our presumptions run deep, not just personally but culturally. Our self-views are based on conceptual fabrications that are deeply rooted in the values, beliefs, and assumptions of our social structure, culture, and personal history. We observe that cultures don't seem to change overnight and we observe the same thing about individuals.

The beliefs upon which self and culture stand are not easily recognized, nor are they easily discarded once we identify them. Remember that both culture and self are created in much the same way—they're the products of many foundation assumptions. These assumptions—

accepting particular ideas to such a degree that they become taken-for-granted realities—give structure to our lives. They are the backdrop for our sense of self and reality, and they offer what seems like solid ground in a world of uncertainty. We may benefit from such structure but we need to recognize that our assumptions are also responsible for most of the limitations and suffering that we experience. What generally goes unnoticed is that they are not facts but merely beliefs and conceptual inventions, and since they are conceptual in nature, they are not necessary in and of themselves.

SUGGESTIONS FOR CONTEMPLATION
Objectification of Concepts

Look into your experience and try to discover anything you hold as real and solid that is actually conceptual. Keep looking into what is generally overlooked and see how much of your experience is conceptually produced.

Some of it might seem self-evident or obvious and considered just an aspect of your life or self or your reality, but look deeply. Are they concepts or are they objects? It might be hard to accept or discern, yet if something you experience isn't objective in nature it is conceptual—no matter how real or solid it seems.

Concentrate on everything in your experience that seems experiential or objective but is actually conceptual. All beliefs, assumptions, interpretations, conclusions, meaning, memories, plans, speculations, extrapolations, ideals, comparisons, good and bad, are conceptual. Regardless of what you think is necessary, get that they are concepts not objects or even experiences.

Concepts, such as beliefs and assumptions, can seem as if they are objectively so, even when they aren't. There are many seemingly real and objective "perceptions" that are actually concepts or are strongly influenced by concept. This is true on many levels and can be very subtle, as we'll see in the next chapter.

OVERLOOKED CONCEPTUAL INFLUENCES
ON EXPERIENCE

To press more deeply into the workings of mind, let's consider how easily concept gets infused and confused with experience and even perceptions. There are many conceptual influences on our experience and perceptions. Some are very subtle and go unnoticed. Let me clarify by starting with a simple exercise.

Image Exercise

To better see this influence, right now take a moment to turn your head from side to side, looking left and then right. What perception gives you the impression that you're moving your head? You can feel your head turning, and your visual field changes, seeing what's to your left and your right.

Now close your eyes and do it again, turn your head from side to side, and notice that you can only feel your head moving. But do you also have an image of your head moving, as though you can "see" your head moving or what it looks like as it moves? Try this with your eyes closed and see what happens, then come back to the book.

The image of your head moving when you have your eyes closed is a concept, not a perception. Since you can't actually see your head moving, you are translating the feeling-sensations into an image and conceptually adding this to your "perception." Fascinating, isn't it?

We mix such images and other conceptual contributions with our perceptive-experience all the time, but we don't notice that they aren't perceptions. Instead, they are conceptual in nature. Just as with our beliefs, all conceptual-activities—thoughts, ideas, speculations, imagination, and much more—influence our sense of reality without our knowing it. Consider how the sensation of turning your head is augmented with a conceptual "image" of that activity. That same interconnectedness between concept and perception is how our beliefs become fused with our perceptions.

If our goal is to free ourselves of the conceptual-activities that create suffering, such a dynamic would obviously need to be sorted out. Since beliefs, assumptions, programming, and speculation are all based on "imagined truths," their influence on our perceptions only muddy the waters.

Perhaps our complex conceptual and social worlds necessitate some blend of concept and perception in order to effectively manage life. This still doesn't mean that the concepts we engage are the healthiest or most effective, or that they are based on fact. This fusion of concepts with perceptions leaves a lot of room for unnecessary and binding fabrications to influence our experience and cause suffering.

What's more, such conceptual influence makes it difficult to discern fact from fiction. In order to align to what's actually occurring, we need to learn to make a distinction between the bare facts—what happened, was said, was done, what is objectively so—and all that is conceptually added to the facts—stories, beliefs, excuses, justifications, meaning, assumptions, suspicions, fantasies, and so on. Gaining clarity here will create a more effective relationship to life.

SUGGESTIONS FOR CONTEMPLATION
Overlooked Conceptual Influence

Work to identify subtle or overlooked conceptual-activities in your overall experience that you take for granted as perceptions. A seamless concept, like the image of moving your head, can seem as if it is an actual perception. See if you can discover others you take for granted as perceptions that are actually concepts added to your experience.

In your experience right now, discover as many conceptual contributions as you can that aren't perceptions but seem like they are or are held as if they are.

Do you get how overlooked concepts can seem like perceptions?

BEING INCOMPLETE

One of the background, and sometimes foreground, forms of suffering we endure is not feeling as if we are whole and complete, that we aren't as we should be. When we look at our experience there is often a sense of not being completely whole, free from dilemma and dissatisfaction. We tend to experience ourselves as unfinished, as needing to be "fixed" somehow, or wanting to have a better life experience than what we have.

This root is the source of many forms of suffering such as dissatisfaction, despair, distress, depression, feeling unworthy, inadequate, flawed, and so on. We often think we are in need of something to make us whole or happy. We live in a world of what we should be but aren't. An overall distinction for this condition could be called being *incomplete*.

Obviously then, being complete would eliminate all of those conditions. Feeling completely whole and happy—without lacking anything you think you or your life should have or be—isn't a common human experience. So one goal we have in our work here is to be complete. In order to do that and have it be real, however, we need to get to the bottom of our self-experience and become more deeply conscious of what we do that fragments our integrity and creates a sense of being incomplete. Toward that end, more foundational work is useful.

CHAPTER TWO

Awakening Overlooked Consciousness

YOU VERSUS YOUR SELF-EXPERIENCE

Most people identify themselves *with* and *as* their characteristic actions and experiences, their beliefs and views, their thoughts and emotions. In order to get free of suffering, we need to change this entrenched view of ourselves. If we stay with the assumption that we *are* what we experience, we can't undo the activities that cause suffering because we then experience *being* our activities instead of *doing* those activities. We also need to change our view from thinking our experience is created by circumstance and instead get that it is something we're doing, not something inflicted upon us.

In order to create some space between "you" and your self-experience, let's look at some metaphors. As in an analogy I used elsewhere, if you were a rock that danced, you might identify yourself as a dancer. But dancing is an activity the rock is doing, it is not the rock itself. This distinction is necessary for our work here, even though it may seem like splitting hairs for most people.

Just so, metaphorically speaking, if you were your body but instead experienced yourself as your style of dress and presentation, you might say "this is who I am" referring to how you look. And indeed, people will know you largely in relation to this show or presentation. But it isn't really you at all. It is what you choose to wear and what you choose to present for others to see, but that doesn't make it you, the body.

Sometimes people think of themselves as the source of their perceptions, that their "consciousness" is the witness or observer of whatever is perceived. This witness or observer distinction can give you space from what you experience and perhaps even provide a way to not identify with whatever is experienced. In that way, it might be useful—shy of a direct consciousness of your real nature—to give you a way to see your "being" as the source of your experiences but not the experiences themselves.

If you are the source of what you experience, then your personality, thoughts, emotional patterns, perceptive faculties, opinions, and the like are activities you are *doing*, not what you are *being*. You may be known through these activities—even though you may not know what the activities themselves really are or what you are if not these activities—but that doesn't make them you.

If you think you are an experience or concept, or that some thought or emotion is needed for you to survive, you won't be able to eliminate those because you think they're you or needed for you to exist. In order to get free of them, you have to be able to make a distinction between you and what you are doing that causes suffering.

Distinction

Before we go on, perhaps I should clarify that I use the word "distinction" in an uncommon way. The dictionary definition suggests that distinction is the difference or contrast between similar things or people. Although this somewhat applies to my use of the word, it is far too limited. What I'm referring to with the word "distinction" is nothing less than *everything* that is experienced in any way. A distinction simply means that whatever we're talking about—an experience, an object, a thought, or anything else—it is exactly that and not something else.

For example, when an object exists it is solely that object, it is not any other object, or the space around it, it is not light or fear or a conundrum. That is how it gets to exist. If it is not distinct from everything else, it can't exist. Do you get how I am using the word?

Everything experienced in any way is a distinction, its mere existence is that distinction. It's important that you understand what I'm saying when I use this word. When it comes to you, *you* need to be *distinct* from your experiences. If you identify yourself as what you experience, you will experience yourself *being* that and so won't be able to separate yourself from the causes of suffering. Now, back to our consideration.

Why does everyone end up going down a road that creates unnecessary suffering? It seems shared unconscious drives that dominate much of our experience push us in this direction, and as mentioned, ignorance is the other reason we continue with ill-fated activities. But what makes this so commonplace for people?

I will pull from a book I am currently working on to further your preparation work here. You may be getting irritated with me drawing from other sources, but I want to give you the best chance at really making a transformation in your experience to end suffering. After this chapter, we will be entering new material that focuses specifically on suffering. But I think if you're best prepared, by understanding some truths to which most people are never exposed, it will empower your efforts. This is taken from more advanced and deeper material that may seem out of reach in this context. But if you can look into these matters, it will serve you in your task to end suffering. Consider it like push-ups: you don't do them for themselves, you do them to help you do other things. So, from *Whereof One Cannot Speak*:

IGNORANCE

Our biological nature makes us learning machines because we begin life from a base of complete ignorance. By design this creates some overlooked existential consequences. Without really understanding the dynamics behind these consequences, we still feel them in the background, and this results in blaming ourselves for deficiencies ill-defined.

Beginning life in complete ignorance and with virtually no skills or capacity to take care of ourselves, we are required to fill in our ignorance and to "learn" the skills necessary to manage life. Beyond what "comes with the package" at birth through genetics, in order to learn basic physical, conceptual, and social abilities we use trial and error and imitation. When it comes to crafting a self—which we really have no inherent idea how to do—we probably also use trial, error, and imitation, trying out various learned human features until some identity begins to form.

Over time, and with much—often forgotten—effort, a great deal of learning and development indeed unfolds. But what's missed in all this is that every piece of knowledge, social skill, understanding, and mental ability that we acquire is invented. Many are adopted inventions from our collective human culture and much is self-invented. For example, clearly language is a cultural invention that we depend on and live within, as are morals, values, traditions, and so on, and none of these existed before they were invented by us collectively. Beliefs, opinions, assumptions, perspectives, and the like tend to be self-invented—but are clearly culturally and socially influenced—and we can see that no belief existed prior to its adoption.

Once again, one of the central inventions that arises in all of this is one's "self." Consider that what you identify with and experience as "you" is something that you crafted and designed. But just like all of the other learning you did, your attention wasn't on the fact that you were creating yourself but on the self you were trying to become.

So without noticing, you remained ignorant of your role in fashioning yourself, since from the beginning your awareness never turned in that direction. The resultant "person" you now identify with simply became your self-experience, with all of your perceptions and attention looking out from this experience as you attempt to manage life from moment to moment. This is another overlooked dynamic.

Even the fundamental consciousness—what we might call "who you really are"—that exists throughout your self-conception is lost within the amalgam of adopted skills, mental activities, and identifiable characteristics you adopted and came to think of as yourself. The primal awareness of your unfettered and unattached source-existence remains hidden from view within your experience until you directly experience who you really are— grasping directly your conscious existence without identity, history, or process. At this point you can begin to contemplate your true nature, or *what* you really are. But that isn't commonly done because, as has been said, your awareness and efforts are naturally devoted to managing life and not getting to the source of your self-experience.

Although we started life in complete ignorance, we've learned a great deal and so naturally assume that all the learning we've done has solved our condition of ignorance. Yet when we look more closely, we can see that it hasn't. This second point may seem to be a false statement on its face because we also assume that our learning is all that *can* be done, and since we seem to know so much, how can it be called ignorance?

Yet when asked what life is, or death is, or what the absolute nature of our existence actually is, or how we came to exist, and so on, we find no direct genuine conscious experience that answers any of these questions. We only find speculation and belief and these do not rise to the level of direct personal consciousness. So it turns out that we are just as ignorant as we were at birth about the foundation realities of self and life and that everything "known" has been learned and so is not an inherent or direct consciousness of these essential matters.

Because of this ignorance and the fact that virtually our whole experience of self and world is adopted or invented, we have a nagging background sense that there is something wrong with our very person. We try to cover up this sense by inserting beliefs and convictions, by gathering more knowledge, by piling up opinions and assumptions, or perhaps by working to become competent and successful. But none of these actions alters our foundation sense that something in ourselves is incomplete and perhaps broken— they simply bury it.

We will look into this domain in more detail later in the book, since it constitutes one of our central forms of suffering.

This condition of existential ignorance doesn't just tend to lead us to a sense of ill-defined personal lacking. It also means in order to fill in the gaps of what's not known we require some other activity to substitute for direct knowledge. This is most often done through adopting beliefs, opinions, convictions, assumptions, and the like.

Beyond these "faux" forms of knowledge, as a community or culture we are further pressed to create inventions that serve to coordinate our interactive efforts and organize our perspectives, thus creating a great deal of our perceived world. Yet these inventions are not known as inventions. No invention is a direct consciousness. Such consciousness is about grasping what's existential and inherent, not what's invented. In this pursuit, it's essential that we know the difference.

INVENTIONS VERSUS DIRECT ENCOUNTER

Although pretty much no one knows it, no matter what beliefs, assumptions, ideas, or even perspectives you have about anything, it is an invention—which means it is not existentially real. Anything that is conceptually generated to serve a purpose cannot be an inherent aspect of existence and obviously it is not objective. Clearly, they were not aspects of existence before their invention. These inventions can vary and can be better or worse, effective or dysfunctional, empowering or debilitating, but they are all still inventions.

This is not to say that you have much of a choice about whether or not to adopt many of these inventions—self, society, culture, language, mind, interpretations, and more—because that's where most of the world in which you live is created. If you want to participate in this world you need to adopt the inventions that make it possible.

Most people have a hard time considering that many experiences such as language and self, mind and society, are inventions and not existential or objective realities. So to tackle this distinction we need to grasp that these "inventions" are actually conceptually generated. But they seem so real, we use them every day and most of our lives are lived through them. It really seems as if language is a natural almost biological function of our reality; self certainly seems self-evident and present as a real and solid experience of our person. How can they be inventions?

To get how this is so, first grasp, as mentioned, that language is invented. At some point it didn't exist and then it did. Also, it only exists when we create it and learn it. But it becomes a constant part of our everyday lives and a familiar and commonplace activity. It also produces so much of the experience that we need in order to relate and live a social life and probably make a living.

Language even becomes the centerpiece of our thinking or mind through our internal dialogue.

The importance of language isn't in question, the fact that it is an invention is the point. We know that phones, refrigerators, cars, and so on are clearly objective inventions, and they are probably also central to our lives even though they are inventions. Conceptual inventions are no less central and no less invented.

It may be harder to grasp that your "self" is an invention. But let me clarify. Here we are not talking about your true or existential nature, nor the existence of your body. In addition to these, you also have an experience of being the "one inside," the conscious entity you identify with. This is largely based on and founded on the idea that you are at the source of your perceptions and is reinforced by the existence of your internal dialogue—which we have already seen is itself an invention. From these kinds of conclusions and assumptions a conceptually generated "experience" of you being a self-residing-within-your-body, and usually inside the head, becomes a taken-for-granted and central aspect that constitutes the core of your self-experience. But I claim this too is an invention. (More on inventing the inner-self later.)

At this point, you may be wondering why this kind of study is necessary and related to suffering. It may all seem too abstract or overly technical and perhaps impractical. These specific distinctions about conceptual inventions may not seem to apply directly but the whole domain of mind that we take for granted does. It is where our suffering is created, and so digging into it, even if in unusual ways, helps provide the understanding necessary to be able to truly change your mind, which is no mean feat.

This point also applies to society. Social reality is invented. Society is based on agreements and values, culture and a collective identity, and in our modern societies many added contributions exist such as a shared language, how we think of mind, the invention of an unconscious mind, human rights, and so on. Again, all of this is conceptually generated to serve a purpose and so is invented.

Grasping that these shared and powerful experiences are inventions is one thing—and we may have no desire to stop using them—but we have many inventions that may well be dysfunctional and unnecessary and cause or contribute to our challenges and pain. If we don't experience them as generated, we can't change or stop doing them. Our perceptive-experience is crafted around many such conceptual inventions, and the resultant behavior we engage because of these determines our relationship to life. Consider this point—don't gloss over what was just said.

Can you see this dynamic operating in your experience? To be clear, these conceptualizations are most often not experienced as minor or superficial activities. They create the experience of your self, your beliefs, your worldview, your self-view, and so on, thus comprising much of your personal reality. But they are actually conceptual-activities created by you. They are inventions but not known as such.

There are many fundamental and agreed upon inventions we share that make our interactions workable—language, politeness, general rules of engagement, shared values, and such. There are also many shared and self-inventions that are dysfunctional— prejudices, judgments, projections, opinions, beliefs, assumptions, jumping to conclusions, values that aren't useful, and so on.

But it can be hard for us to sort out which is which in our own case, since whether useful or dysfunctional both are accepted as our self-experience and view of reality. Yet with critical inspection and detached observation we can begin to discern which personal mental activities are detrimental to our overall well-being and growth.

Many of these self-inventions are found in our beliefs and assumptions, perspectives, and cosmologies—"cosmology" is a word I use to loosely refer to our personal views about how the world and reality work. Beliefs that aren't true are rarely useful or effective. Beliefs that limit and damage us in some way are dysfunctional and should be dropped.

In some cases, these damaging beliefs might be rather obvious, such as a belief that you are worthless, or that all others are evil and liars, and the like. Rationally, you can see such beliefs will limit and degrade your experience of life. But even though you might be able to recognize that some belief is disempowering, you may not be able to drop it easily because you still believe it. See the rub? Only when you can get that it is something you are doing and that you don't have to do it can you drop it.

There will be beliefs that seem justified and serving self-preservation that are neither. These can be beliefs you're attached to simply because you want to be—even if unconsciously—not because they empower you. But this reality is overlooked. You may well also have cosmologies or perspectives that darken your world or push you into a dysfunctional corner. But without these invented "realities" a much more open relationship to life with many more possibilities could be available to you.

To pursue this introspective work, one question you can ask is: Does this "invention" (belief, view, assumption, perspective, opinion, etc.) really empower and free me or does it limit and degrade my experience? Remember, everything you experience should be up for inspection. Within this conceptually invented domain it is the choices you make that create the degree to which your personal world is successful or satisfying. Most people have no idea that they can change long-held beliefs and assumptions. For them, it seems that such things are fixed and simply a reflection of what's real. But they aren't. You can stop generating any invention.

Yet no matter how much you change or drop, or how great and powerful your inventions are, they will never be objectively existent and, given they are invented, ultimately they can't be inherently real. Their reality exists as an activity you are doing, not something that just *is*.

Pressing Beyond Inventions

Whether ultimately real or not, when we investigate our mental and physical domains thoroughly—as is touched upon in the books *The Genius of Being* and *Zen Body-Being*—we discover an incredible brilliance to its design and complexity. Yet most people spend their lives without such exploration and merely take much for granted about the world in which they live. Even so, the human brain alone is far more ingenious than most of the thinking that comes out of it.

The complexity and interconnected intelligence that seems to comprise a bee colony or a computer pales in comparison to the human brain. And yet we only access understanding of the brilliant design of the brain indirectly through science and research, and the end product of this effort is a knowledge that takes the form of ideas, concepts, and images about what's true. We don't access it personally by directly experiencing our very own brains.

Imagine what might be different in our world if we did. In order to do so, however, we'd be required to match the intelligence, complexity, and effectiveness of our own brains within our conscious experience. We assume we can't do this because we don't do it.

Yet we have to admit that at least in the case of our own brains, selves, and bodies, we are quite close to and intimately connected to them. What's to say we can't become conscious of the real nature or intricate dynamics that exist in the very place we experience *being*?

Such a notion isn't considered possible by our culture, but possibilities exist outside the inventions of any culture. Consider that whatever you are, you can become directly conscious of because it *is* you; and whatever life and existence are, you can also become directly conscious of because you are alive and you do exist. These would be direct encounters and not merely inventions.

A direct encounter is quite different from most of what occurs in the domain of our minds and experience. It is not having an idea, belief, assumption, conclusion, conviction, image, conjecture, feeling, perception, sense, knowledge, or any other form of experience that comes about through indirect means. It may be hard to understand but indirect means the "information" coming into your consciousness is not the thing-in-itself but a representation, or an effect of some activity that is independent from the subject even though it seems to be related to the subject.

All perception, thought, and experience is indirect. This is just saying the perceptive-experience you have is not the same as the thing-in-itself. For example, when you see something, you assume—and live as if—the perception is the same thing as what's viewed. But what's true about that sight is the perception itself is a function of light bouncing off an object and you interpreting the light. This means the "data" gathered by the light stimulating nerves in the eye is funneled through interpretation and association to make sense of it. Any one of those activities makes it indirect. Without the light, you have no experience of the thing whatsoever and even with the light you don't have any information that isn't carried by light. Yet no matter how many indirect perceptions, concepts, or other activities are added to the mix, it will still be indirect—because it is.

When it is direct, it isn't dependent upon anything but the subject itself because it *is* the subject itself. See the difference? This is not a common distinction. For most people, everything perceived or experienced is indirect. The only exception might be having an insight where the subject hits one's consciousness without a middleman. This, however, is still a function of mind and not the true nature of the subject, but it indicates the direction of a direct encounter.

We can divide this direct-encounter distinction into two possibilities. One is a direct consciousness of the absolute or true nature of some aspect of existence. This is also called an "enlightenment," what I usually refer to as direct consciousness. The other is gleaning what something is or is about in a relative sense. We could call this a direct encounter in the relative domain. Here we can grasp an invention *as* an invention even while we are using it. This is a very different perspective and freedom from just living inside of it. When we personally experience the truth of the subject and get what it is for-itself we could also call this a direct encounter.

Basically, personally grasping the truth of something directly, not based on hearsay, belief, conjecture, or anything else, could be called a direct encounter or direct experience in the relative domain. Becoming conscious of the true nature of any aspect of existence—self, other, objective reality, life—is a direct consciousness of the absolute truth. Neither of these are inventions or subjective musings. In both cases the direction is toward what's true.

We might struggle with this kind of stuff, wondering why does it matter if we have direct or indirect encounters? Yet it is the possibility of direct experience, although seemingly obscure, that gives us access to experiencing reality in a new way. Since one of our goals is to end suffering, we need this ability. If we can only live within the accepted indirect encounters and invented realities that make up our world, we are at a loss to tackle such a new possibility as ending suffering. On the other hand, to achieve it we need to know what suffering is and how it is created, and this can only occur when we put ourselves directly into the matter.

I touched on the idea that our experience of being an inner-self is an invention. This is a very unusual assertion and so requires more explanation. These next sections may be appear unbelievable or even impossible assertions on their surface and can be challenging to grasp, but see if you can directly experience what is really being asserted.

THE INNER-SELF IS AN INVENTION

Where do you locate yourself in your experience? It seems that almost all humans experience their "private" selves, their inner self-awareness, as residing inside their bodies and usually inside their heads. Can you find this sense of an inner-self right now in your experience? This location is usually taken for granted as the "seat" or "place" where you exist.

When you talk to yourself or have a thought, where does that take place? Is that the place where "you" reside? Do you experience yourself as occupying a private inner world, an internal state to which only you are privy? Isn't this where you locate "you" as a conscious entity? Isn't this place and this "one" the most important and necessary living element for you?

I've talked elsewhere about living inside and why it seems real, but the real nature of this seemingly existential condition is rarely grasped. As the title of this section states, the whole notion, perception, and experience of an internal self is an invention. How can that be? It seems to be self-evident and obvious. But we fail to notice that the reason it is obvious is because we assume it to be existentially true and necessary, and this assumption creates the very experience that makes it self-evident.

But ask yourself, can you find this "one behind the scenes" that you never really see? If you have done lots of contemplation you can attest that try as you might to find this one, you can't. Why is that? You may keep assuming you can find it but are just unable. You still can't find it. This is because it isn't there!

But don't take my word for it, give it a try, and a try, and a try, until you are convinced for yourself. You can experience what is there and you can become consciousness of who and what you really are, but you can't find what's not there. That's because this inner-self is an invention, and it's not shared by all creatures.

It shouldn't be too hard to imagine that a tree or single-cell organism has no such internal world or notion of an inner-self— even though we tend to project the inner-self notion onto all living things because we assume it is the essence of all creatures, just as we assume it's an essential aspect of ourselves. Yet without standing on such assumptions we can also imagine that a tree has no self or mind and no inner world.

It isn't difficult to imagine the tree has no internal dialogue because we experience it as having no language. Just so, an animal that has no conceptually constructed language also has no need nor impulse for an inner-self or the notion of an internal state to arise. We should be able to see it living simply as a body perceiving its environment, which defines its world.

So it also shouldn't be too difficult to conjure up the idea that at one point humans themselves had no such isolated sense of an inner-self. If we extend this to the idea of having no "mind"—or internal state—this may be harder to imagine because we assume mind is fundamental to the human condition. Yet consider that long ago humans, or human predecessors, had no language, so like the tree or animal they could not be talking to themselves, and that activity is a major contributor to creating the notion of being inside and having a mind. Couple that with a total lack of wonder about what might be at the source of perception, we can see no inclination to create a notion that anything other than the body itself is perceiving.

Once again, we see that prior to inventing the distinction of mind there is only a body and the activities of the body. We can imagine that at some past point for us, like the animals, knowledge of anything inside the body was absent and likely of little concern. If the body was opened up we'd find only organs and other physical features. So where is this internal state or inner person to be found?

It's not there, nor is it experienced unless it is invented. But how can such a clear and obvious experience that pretty much everyone shares be an invention and in this way not inherently or existentially real? The fact that everyone shares in this experience might make it seem like it must be inherent in and a function of the mere existence of being human, like an organ that is a given. Yet pretty much everyone shares the experience of language and we can see that language is an invention and also something that had to be learned by each individual. Therefore, just because experiences are shared doesn't make them inherent.

So how does this inner-self get created in such a nonrandom way? In the ways I've already described elsewhere, but to briefly recap: A thought forms that one's location is at the source of the perceptive faculties and resides as an immaterial "object" within the body somewhere. This "immaterial object from which consciousness arises" remains assumed rather than inspected and becomes held as the real-you. Yet when you begin to thoroughly inspect and attempt to directly experience who you are, you discover that you can't find this self-object, try as you might. The reason you can't find it is that it doesn't exist, and it isn't you. It is an invented assumption that forms into what seems like an experience and, just like the assumptions of self and mind, this assumption has spread widely throughout humanity.

You perceive a body but only assume there is an unseen internal entity at the source of or "behind" bodily perceptions—this internal self is probably seen as either an aspect of the body or as distinct from but living within the body. When deeply inspected, both body and perception can produce fascinating results—you can discover many interesting and overlooked dynamics there. But no matter where you look in the objective world or what you find, this search still doesn't reveal an inner-self.

If you stop assuming the shared conclusions drawn from imagining that you are located behind the perceptive organs and associated with the reproduction of your own voice within and simply stand on objective reality as the foundation, you can see the real nature of this inner-self. Stop assuming and generating the activity that makes it so and no inner-self exists.

If not inside, where is the self? If we hold that this inner-self shares the same source as the mind, we have to ask: where is this mind? But we will soon learn that mind is also an invention, so that doesn't help. If not simply a body, where are you?

That can remain an unanswered question for now and still we are able to recognize the false nature of the inner-self—that it is an activity we are doing rather than a fact of our essential existence. Think about it, if you didn't have any thought or concept that you are within, if you didn't assume a location behind perceptive organs, what would you experience? If the inner-self is an experience produced by these activities, its location still has to be assumed or just remain unknown. If we speak of you—as in your true nature—rather than any self-experience you have, this too either remains unknown or is directly experienced as nothing and nowhere at all.

Even within the relative world, we don't need an inner-self in order for us to exist or to live successfully. Living within this assumption as if it's an essential aspect of oneself isn't useful. Perhaps inventing and using a distinction such as "mind" might create certain benefits. With this invention we create a new domain of distinctions and relate to matters in new ways that produce new results. Whether these additions are beneficial or not depends on what they are and what they do. But it is never beneficial to accept even such an invention as "mind" as an existential reality rather than what it is, which is the creation of a new context in which to hold experience.

On the other hand, being ignorant of our assumption of being an inner-self-object doesn't appear to have any benefits but does have many negative consequences. Primarily, it defines the life and world that is lived as yourself, thus making your self-sense smaller and more isolated. It leads to much mischief and a detachment from being responsible for your private inner "behavior," tending to reduce your sense of responsibility and overall integrity. Living with such a distinction isn't necessary, but if you do, I recommend that you at least fully experience it as an invention and not as an inherent aspect of your existence—and if you're going to live inside this inner space at least "clean up your room."

THE NATURE OF MIND

Since mind seems so central to our self-experience let's take a deeper look at its nature. It might sound like an absurd statement to say that the mind doesn't really exist. But difficult as it might be to grasp, like the inner-self, mind is also an invention. If we can see how the private inner world in which we live is created, it shouldn't be out of the question to consider mind might also be a creation. But this could take some contemplation to break free of accepted assumptions.

Although culturally we accept mind as part of our experience and existence, it's good to note that no one has ever seen one. Consider the possibility that before the distinction of "mind" was invented by ancient cultures, there was no "mind." People didn't perceive it, think about it, talk about it, or experience it in any way. We like to think that "mind" still existed and people were just ignorant of it. But is that true? Since we don't know what mind is, it might be that it really doesn't exist except as a created distinction.

Try to imagine a world in which you had no "experience" of mind—no thought of mind, no word "mind," no reference to mind, no idea of a "place" where thoughts and emotions "reside," no concept at all that there is such a thing. What would life and experience be like without the distinction mind? Mind is an invention in our perceptive-experience that serves to indicate and create the notion of an "internal state."

If we can recognize mind as a created context for experience, we see that this allows for a new domain of distinctions that didn't occur before this invention. The content of this context are the distinctions that constitute all conceptual-activities—ideas, beliefs, concepts, fantasies, imagination, memory, emotions, intuition, and so on. Even our reference to "the mind" (as if something is there) is content, not the context of which I speak. And neither the context nor the content is an object.

We may attribute the workings of mind to the brain but in our experience mind isn't an object, it's an activity. We tend to assume, without much thought, that there is somehow a "mind-object" filled with "conceptual-objects." Yet in our experience, we only find mind as activities, not objects. When we grasp the nature of mind, we see that nothing is objectively there. As I asked in *The Book of Not Knowing* (11:1), "If we were to open up your skull and look into your brain to search for the number four, do you think we would find a '4' in there? No, we would find a lot of tissue and blood."

It might be difficult to grasp what might have existed prior to inventing the idea and distinction we call mind. We live within an assumption that everything we experience was an aspect of being human from the beginning, and people before us were just ignorant of these things. But this isn't true at all. Many human experiences and whole perceived realities didn't exist until they were created at some point.

For example, again, consider that at one time humans had no language. Without language, there are activities that can't be done—such as speaking, symbolizing, writing, recording, counting, and so on. There are also understandings, beliefs, assumptions, interpretations, and experiences that just cannot take place without language.

We think of language as simply giving words to known phenomena or observable things. But without language where is the known or observed phenomena that is "lying," or "philosophy," or "betrayal," or "accountability," or "clarity," or "art," or "metaphor," or "internal dialogue" (so often confused with "thinking" itself), or "promise," and so on? Without the context and so content of language these and many more cannot be observed, since they can't exist without it.

They weren't an aspect of reality waiting to be labeled; they simply weren't an aspect of reality. This is hard to understand, especially since people make a huge assumption that their current experience of the world is a reflection of what has always been, and so have a hard time experiencing or even thinking about anything outside of or prior to that assumption.

What we might see as "observable phenomena" existing prior to language—such as objects and movement—are still influenced and altered within our experience *by* language. Obviously, any influence or alteration that has occurred through the invention and application of language did not exist before language, and so that experience wouldn't have existed. If this is true of language, why not mind? Can you see the parallel between the creation of language and the creation of mind?

Perhaps it will help to look at a relatively new set of distinctions. Consider all the concepts that originally began with Freud that we unthinkingly bandy about in Western culture. Whether or not one embraces his ideas, after barely a century, it's nearly impossible to think "pre-Freud." To paraphrase the poet W. H. Auden (from as early as 1939): *To us Freud is no longer a person, but a whole climate of opinion under which we conduct our different lives.* Did "unconscious mind" exist for people before the term was popularized by Freud? Obviously not in people's experience.

The so-called "unconscious mind" was created pretty much in the same way as mind. That means neither existed prior to their creation. I remember a story told by a graduate student of psychology. He had a professor that fit the image of a typical Freudian with accent and all. One day when the student went into the teacher's office, the professor said, "Do you believe in zee unconscious mind?" The student was taken aback, knowing that the entire domain of psychology is based on this idea. So he said, "Of course." The professor, looking over his glasses, said, "I don't."

Imagine before the notion that there exists a part of the mind inaccessible to one's daily experience was proffered, no one thought there was anything in their experience that wasn't known and obvious. It might seem like this aspect of mind was there but just overlooked, but is that true? Perhaps it's just a new way to look at experience, like the distinction of mind itself.

Have you ever seen a mind? No, no one has. It is not something observable and exists only when the distinction of "mind" is made. In other words, you might say that the body exists as something observable and inherent to being human, but why say there is mind? Without language, for example, there would be no internal dialogue, no abstract references, no symbolism, no inferences, no abstract philosophical or psychological "thinking," and so on. How much of that is entirely a product of the context of mind? Well, all of it.

Imagine what it might be like if you lived in a world where there was no distinction called "mind." You may see people all around, and perhaps even talk to them and interact with them, but where would you see or observe a mind at work? You wouldn't. Currently, you imagine there is a mind operating behind people's actions, but without this distinction their actions would simply be their actions. Without the distinction of mind, there would be no experience of mind.

So, again, you may ask, "but doesn't mind exist even if we don't make such a distinction?" OK, *where*? You are postulating that mind is some *thing* that exists somewhere and awaits our discovery. But that assumption only arises from the experience in which mind already exists as an aspect of being human. Mind isn't an object, it is an activity that has to be created and can only occur as activities of mind after the context of mind has been created in which to hold these activities as its content. Even if some activity occurs as a fact, that this activity is mind doesn't arise into experience or awareness unless the context and distinction of mind is created. In various forms, the distinction of mind or something similar has been made by almost all cultures, but even these aren't all the same distinction.

This distinction can't be made until a new context is created. This context could itself be called "Mind." Yet we need to consider that the context or possibility that is created isn't what we think of as mind. Instead, it is the "space" in which we can create the distinction of a mind as we know it today. It is the possibility, created by humans, that there is something going on in our experience that is not attributable to the body and its activities.

Consider that, prior to the context of mind, something like perception would be considered a bodily function, such as the eye "seeing" or the ear "hearing." There is no need for mind there. Perhaps, if a thought arose, it wouldn't be a "thought," it would be the body knowing or reacting and would not only be different from what we currently think but would probably go unnoticed in itself, rather like breathing or a burp. Are you starting to get a picture here?

If you're formulating a picture of what I'm talking about, this will be held as a function of mind. I'm not saying that this picture couldn't exist prior to the invention of the context of mind, only that if it did, it wouldn't be held as a mental activity but as a function of the body, or whatever distinctions are made and identified with as the human experience. Do you see that you can't say "*just* making a distinction within your experience" as if it's an inconsequential activity? Or that there is such a thing as the fact of experience that we only "decide" to divide up into new distinctions?

The core principles of the human condition are very difficult to understand because we have such a hard time grasping anything outside our own fabricated "reality," which has been built, by the way, upon millennia of humankind's conceptual inventions. But consider, beyond this consideration, what was the reality prior to any created distinction? Not just mind but what is reality without all the inventions we've developed over the millennia? Quite a contemplation. I doubt that saying more will add much clarity, so I'll leave it there.

Before starting our direct study of ending suffering, I want to press a little more to help increase your ability to make distinctions in your experience about what is you and what is not. To be able to get free of suffering you'll need to experience yourself as distinct from what you do that causes it. Experiencing yourself as a being that creates thoughts, and not as the thoughts themselves, allows you to stop creating thoughts that are dysfunctional.

If you've worked with me before in any form you know I do not support you believing in anything I say or what anyone says. So you are invited to set out to experience these assertions for yourself, not to believe them. If you can't do that, for now, just consider them as possibilities, and for our work here, try to use them to create some space in how you hold yourself that serves to separate yourself from the concepts you are doing. Unless you've worked with me before, I would recommend you skip over this last section, because it is likely to be seen as either bullshit or fantasy and I don't support either. It stands on more advanced considerations and may not be understood correctly. If you read it without a sufficient background with me, please consider it just a crash course in possibilities to contemplate and not something to believe.

DISTINCTIONS WITHIN THE SELF

Now I am about to go down a tricky road. I'm going to talk about different distinctions or aspects within your experience of self. The tricky part isn't so much making these distinctions but that they might turn into some form of hierarchy and fall into being thought of as a diagrammatic form like concentric circles or some such. Why is this a danger? Certainly, viewing a diagram and ordering a hierarchy makes things clear to the mind. But that's the danger. It cannot be accurate.

All models are wrong,
but some are useful.
GEORGE BOX

This conundrum is a bit similar to the debate that arose many centuries ago when certain aspects of the Christian community wanted to paint Bible stories on the walls inside religious buildings. At the time, most people couldn't read, and this group wanted the stories to be seen. The other side of the debate asserted that nothing can represent God, and even applying a name takes us further from the reality, and if these stories were made into cartoon form they would become simplistic and misunderstood. The painting people won. So now we have a God as a white-bearded man in the clouds, and so on. Do you think such an image forwards understanding the nature of God or diminishes it? You can guess which side of the argument I'm on.

That said, I will venture down a road that will be like the paintings in some way, but please don't hear each distinction being made as equal to the others or of the same nature, nor as a hierarchy. They are distinctions we can make in our experience of being. None are more or less important in our composition. Remember we make many distinctions about a rock in color and weight and shape, but that doesn't mean these distinctions are separate from each other or the rock.

Our first distinction is your true or absolute nature. This is what you actually are at the source of your existence. It is the true nature of you as a conscious entity. This nature is without element, it is not relative or formed. This nature is actually not a distinction, because it isn't relative. We simply make a distinction so we can speak about it. Because of this your nature is actually open-ended. But you can only come to this consciousness directly; believing in such hearsay is worthless and inaccurate.

Yet when you become conscious of this nature you will make a distinction to represent it in your experience. At this point it is best to simply acknowledge that it can't be defined or pinned down. When you have this direct consciousness, you may or may not realize that the distinction you make is not your nature itself, but you will still make a distinction since that is how the mind works.

Second, we might say that from this nature arises a "one" that you are. Yet this one is also not formed except that it is the conscious entity you identify being prior to any personality or characteristics. This is "who" you actually are. It is difficult to imagine this distinction because whenever we think of a "one" it usually occurs as a thing, and a thing is always objective and formed, even if we think of it as an "immaterial" object.

In grasping who you are, it is you but there is nothing added to that. Who you are refers to the one that you are, but there is no other quality than it is you as a conscious entity. Directly experiencing this one isn't commonplace because we live within the person that we identify, which defines us as an individual, and so we usually aren't conscious of the unbridled entity we are before any identity forms.

Now the distinctions become tricky in a different way because we enter the world of a "person" having specific characteristics as an individual. These various aspects are interconnected and build upon one another as well as influence each other. This third distinction refers to the person that is experienced beyond who you are that is formed into a particular individual.

We could consider this existentially or psychologically. Existentially, we see that we identify with a human and an individual, the form of which is rather unimportant. Personally, or psychologically, we see how this individual is unique or specific. For you, this "base" person may not be seen clearly for what it is because you will be strongly identified with your social persona. But the base-person is the individual that is deemed the one that needs to persist and survive.

The fourth, and last, distinction is your social persona, which isn't just how you act in the company of others, but what you think about yourself even when alone. Even when alone your self-view is determined largely by elements created only because of the social domain—being selfish or generous, worthless or superior, your level of self-esteem, how you see yourself as a person, and so on. Such values are all only possible through the creation of a social domain. Here, the self that needs to survive is modified to manage social interactions, and so survive in a social context.

Selfish versus Social

To look at this from a different viewpoint consider your "base" person— the third distinction—as your "selfish" self, and the fourth distinction as your "social" self. The selfish-self, however, will also be seen primarily within a social construct. A social perspective has to be based upon something that can be related to and judged; this is the base-self I referred to. Beyond the social, however, the selfish person you are is the one that at the core you revert to when the shit hits the fan—the most solid identity and characteristic way that you are.

It is the foundation-you, what might be conventionally confused with who you are. It is the "way you are" at the core of your person, with particular characteristics prior to or independent from social concerns. It is very hard to communicate what I'm seeing as this foundation-person because, again, it is prior to what we know and love as the social person you manifest as—even though it is also strongly influenced by social concerns. Perhaps the most fundamental aspect of this base is selfishness.

This is also hard to grasp because we don't want to think of ourselves as selfish, although in the privacy of our inner self-world we know that we are. But it is even more challenging because the judgment that selfish is wrong is a social convention, and we begin forming ourselves in relation to a social environment at the earliest stages of life. But this base is independent of social concerns except how our survival depends on others.

The selfish-self is not necessarily something one wants others to see, and so it often remains hidden from view, veiled behind the "act" that is put on to seem socially acceptable. Although there is a difference between the selfish-self and the social-self, both of these self-identities are driven by the same impulse—self-survival. One is focused on what is thought to serve the individual, and the other is what is thought to serve one's social life, trying to manage how others see and relate to you.

Can you find these aspects within you? You have selfish impulses that sometimes you act on. But sometimes you suppress or keep them hidden because they conflict with your social concerns—being accepted by others, protecting your self-image, managing what others think about you, ergo what you think about yourself in that context, and so on. Social interactions are very often important to us in many ways, and we want to "survive" in that world as well as in the world outside of or independent of social interactions.

We always modify our behaviors to balance between these two forces—the selfish and the social. Some of us tend to lean more toward the selfish and some tend strongly toward the social, but everyone has both of these going on. We see examples of those seen as being far more self-oriented and not very "social" creatures. This could show up as being selfish, devious, arrogant, or it could show up more like being self-confident, independent, unaffected by social fears, or whatever. These two versions are seen as negative or positive through a social lens, and this is determined by how our behavior bothers or impresses others.

On the other hand, we see examples of people who are extremely social, crafting their behavior around how others see them, striving to be seen a certain way, engaging in many relationships, needing to be a part of community, and so on. Again, this could be seen as a good thing or as dependency. For some it could show up as strong and confident, whereas for others it might show up as weakness and desperation.

Regardless of variety, the distinction here is that our "selfish" person is about taking care of ourselves regardless of the needs or thoughts of others, and our social person lives in relationship to the thoughts of others. We exist as both, and simply balance between these two aspects of ourselves.

Don't confuse reputation or behavior patterns as necessarily indicative of the selfish-self; they may or may not be. An aggressive or surly person might be basically unsure of themselves and fearful within; a positive and gregarious person could be avoiding depression because they feel a lot of deep self-negativity. It might take some looking into to ascertain the base of a person outside of their social persona, especially when it comes to yourself.

Again, it should be noted that all characteristics are seen through the lens of a social context and judged accordingly. But looking into your base makeup is best done without any social judgments. So, for example, the selfish nature would not be seen as bad but as a commitment to self-survival. Consider that babies are very selfish, but we don't expect them to be otherwise. We rarely see them as bad because we know they haven't developed their social skills yet and so view them as innocent. It may be difficult, but take a moment and try to see your selfish-self outside of social judgments.

What I'm referring to here as the selfish-self is prior to social interactions—but not independent of them, since this base is also crafted in relation to others. Social interactions are one of the key aspects of our environment we must relate to in order to manage life successfully. Our base person will influence our social interactions because this is what we think of ourselves deep down, even if we try to keep it hidden. The experience of our basic or selfish-self will also be judged in a social context, so it all loops and intertwines. The point here is there's a fundamental way of being that influences all else that follows. See? It's tricky.

Briefly, beyond Who and What we really are, once we have formed into an individual person, we run down a road of unfolding into a base character wed to an uncognized mind, and the actions and behaviors that result from interactions with others form the person and personality that we experience, and this shows up as the "acts" we adopt that becomes our social persona. After who we really are, the vast majority of all this is conceptual and leads to a great deal of mischief that causes unnecessary suffering.

PART II

෴

Getting Free from Unnecessary Suffering

Does not man, perhaps, love something besides well-being?
Perhaps he is just as fond of suffering? Man is sometimes
extraordinarily, passionately, in love with suffering, and
that is a fact.

DOSTOEVSKY

Our ignorance of the domain of the realities we've touched on so far creates overlooked consequences in ways that may be hard to see. These overlooked consequences generate mental activities that have a profound effect on our entire life experience. For example, as we saw, one of the realities that act as a foundation for our experience is living in a private inner world. From this taken-for-granted assumption, the activities that arise from this inner world often generate a considerable amount of personal suffering. All of this suffering is unnecessary.

I invite you to pay careful attention to what's to come. There are many very powerful communications in this section. Truly grasping them can transform your experience of life. It is actually possible for you to end all unnecessary suffering—and almost all of it is unnecessary. But in order to take it into action you need to incorporate what's being said into your experience.

Having worked through the mind-bending assertions made so far—most of which probably don't seem very related to your practical experience of life—has hopefully prepared you to better tackle ending suffering. This is because ending suffering requires grasping how you create it. But such an understanding and ability is not commonplace. Getting what you are doing that generates suffering allows you to stop doing it. I think this knowledge should be broadly available and commonplace for all of humanity, but so far, it's not.

> *Don't Take Anything Personally. Nothing others do is because of you. What others say and do is a projection of their own reality. When you are immune to the opinions and actions of others, you won't be the victim of needless suffering.*
>
> DON MIGUEL RUIZ

CHAPTER THREE

Conceptualizing versus Being

HAVE YOU NOTICED YOU DESIRE experiences and circumstances that aren't present? Take a look. How often do you find yourself wanting experiences such as pleasure, safety, a better life, a sense of permanence, and so on? Perhaps you desire an imagined "life" that you currently don't have. Notice where these "experiences" live. They are only imagined. If you look closer, you can find an image or idea preceding each of these forms of suffering.

Why would I call them forms of suffering? They seem promising, something to strive for to make life better. How can that be suffering? Every desire and mental-emotional need—longing for something not occurring, focusing on something better than what you experience—are based on pain and dissatisfaction. Whatever you desire confesses it is something you don't have and that what you do have isn't good enough or complete. But the dynamic I am pointing to is much more specific and grounded than the rather abstract, albeit true, general notion that desire creates suffering.

Now, take a breath. Don't leap to the conclusion that you know what I'm talking about quite yet and end up defending desire as essential for your well-being, or freaking out about the idea that desire might be taken away from you. Consider, I might be making a distinction yet to be revealed. Keep an open mind and this will be laid out in detail, but it will take some time to fully understand. This is a big matter that won't fit into a quick sound bite.

This form of suffering is pretty much unique to humans because it is generated by a complex of conceptualizations. Worried about something? What has to happen in order to worry? You must create the idea and imagination that something not yet occurring could go wrong. Dissatisfied with life? Again, you must create the idea that life could and should be some other way than what you experience. Feeling unworthy or worthless? Among other things, besides having the concept that "worth" somehow applies to your existence, you have to compare yourself to something imagined that doesn't exist. Examples can go on and on.

You only have to look at your experience as you live life to find examples of forms of suffering from minor or subtle to major and dramatic. To be clear, dissatisfaction is a form of suffering, being irritated is a form of suffering, feeling unease is a form of suffering, negatively judging yourself is a form of suffering, feeling less than is a form of suffering. Getting the idea? Don't overlook the many forms of suffering that just seem to be taken-for-granted parts of life.

We've seen that many concepts dominate our experience and a great deal gets overlooked because it just seems as if they're necessary aspects of life. For example, there is much for us to desire. Try to bring to mind everything you desire, from romance to tasty food, having a nice experience to avoiding conflict, being successful in life to having a better job. Be creative and notice that you also desire not to feel pain or discomfort. See how much that expands your list. Notice desire is never about what *is* occurring; it is about what is imagined.

If concept is everything that isn't currently objectively occurring, using your previous work on concept, discern how much of your "experience" is actually conceptual. Notice much of life is lived in "idea-land." You worry, long for, seek, desire, fear, mentally and emotionally struggle, and so on, and all these and many more are based solely on ideas, concepts—on figments of mind you generate and think are real. Again, at this point you may be fretting or jumping to conclusions—these are among the activities that create suffering by the way—but hang in there, it will all become grounded and clear as the communication unfolds.

To get a better handle on how much suffering you create solely though conceptualizing, again notice that most creatures, like a swan or rabbit, have none of this form of suffering. They have no idea that there could be more to life or that it's possible to have any other experience than what they are having. They don't imagine anything not perceived. They have no idea of a "better" experience or world, nor do they suffer the idea of death or loss. They have little to no social complications, communication problems, misunderstandings, imagining what others think about them, the meaning behind a sentence or an action, and so on.

Notice they don't suffer so much of what we suffer. They don't worry or fret like we do, or fear the future, or crave anything not available. They don't imagine that they are somehow flawed or less than they should be. Remember the three-legged dog? Such objective maladies in these creatures don't seem to produce any disturbance at all because of them. Notice, or imagine, the difference between our experience and theirs and the degree of suffering they don't seem to have, simply because they don't have the complex conceptual "ability" that for us tends to run amok.

Of course, we like to think the simple creatures are just ignorant and we are so much smarter and can do so much more. But seriously consider: What is the "more" we are doing? What in this "more" is unhealthy, ineffective, and causes suffering? We don't usually consider this reality and proceed with our "more," ignorant of all the activities that generate unnecessary suffering, thinking it is all necessary and simply part of the same package that gave us our superpowers to begin with.

Is it possible that the Garden of Eden story had something to do with this new power? The adoption of some activity that creates a new domain of ability but at the same time also creates the misery and suffering that humans so frequently endure. What Adam and Eve didn't get is they could create the powerful aspects of concept and yet avoid the idiocy that creates so much unnecessary suffering. But one step at a time. We'll get to how to do that later, after we understand the foundation reality that makes it possible.

Another thing such creatures provide as a contrast is the fact they have no notion that there is something true that is unknown or that they are going to die. Their present experience is all that is for them, and nothing more. Because of all this they don't suffer, especially mentally and emotionally, nearly as much as humans. Their desires are likely incredibly basic and immediate, simply handling physical survival from moment to moment. As a result, they are much calmer and more at peace than almost any human.

Real life always and only occurs in present time, as what is experienced in this moment. Again, notice it is *always* now; no matter what happens, it happens now. There is no future or past except as a concept, and although this concept might seem to arise now, it isn't about now, it is about what "isn't," not what *is*. I use the word "isn't," in this case, to refer to mental activities since they are fabricating an imagined reality that is not actually what *is* as an objective reality.

Real Life

Real life only occurs in and as what "is"—which is life as it is actually and objectively lived. This is where life factually occurs. For example, breathing, eating, walking, speaking, writing, laughing, kissing, frowning, hitting, sitting, and so on are physical and biological activities that constitute life as it's lived. These are what keep us alive and make a real difference in life. I call this "real life" to ground this distinction in the objective actions where biological life actually takes place.

The term "real life" exists as a contrast to all the mental-emotional activities that arise within our minds. This world of imagination doesn't make a difference in real life, except for the influence it can have on our physiology and behavior. Such activities as worrying, imagining, thinking, desiring, longing, talking to oneself, fantasizing, judging, disapproving, believing, and on and on, exist only as inner conceptual-activities and often as turmoil. They only make a difference in real life insofar as they influence the objective actions we take because of them or produce some physiological side effect in the body or nervous system such as stress. Real life is where life is actually lived, not all this nonsense that goes on in our minds.

Life is what happens to you while you're busy making other plans.

JOHN LENNON

It is crucial in this work to experientially be able to make the distinction between everything that constitutes conceptual-life versus objective-life. Without this experiential distinction, you can't proceed to end suffering. Notice that when you have all of your attention on what *is*—on life unfolding in present time, no matter what it is—the vast majority of your suffering and dissatisfaction evaporates. If you grasp that the huge world of what *isn't*—existing only in imagination and concept—is actually *not* occurring as objective reality and is not an experience of life in this moment, you can begin the process of letting go of *isn't* in favor of *is*.

Some of the world of *isn't* is easy to see as unreal—fantasies, imagination, daydreaming, and so on. We know these activities to be figments of mind and not a part of real life as I define it. Yet much of *isn't* infects and infests the experience of *is* and goes unnoticed for what it is. In many ways, we endow *isn't* with way too much power and assume it has the same status as what *is* or real life.

These conceptual-activities simply seem to be necessary aspects of present life when in fact they aren't. Some of the conceptual-activities that are disguised as real life—but actually aren't—are taken-for-granted beliefs and belief systems, assumptions, life plans, ideals, a sense of destiny, comparisons to others, personal self-agendas, cosmologies or worldviews, life stories, past traumas, the desire for something not present, needs, self-judgments, and so on.

If you make a distinction between what is—an experience of what is really occurring as life in present time and only in present time and only what is objectively or really occurring without the influence of concepts related to things not present—and what isn't, you can separate out what isn't from what is and experience being in life as it is, not life as it isn't—or should be, or might be, or could be. Consider this contrast.

Again, probably from time to time you have come close to a simple and present experience of simply "being" in this moment. I suspect you enjoyed that experience. So why would you spend so much time in and devote so much effort to the plethora of ideas and imaginings that create unnecessary suffering? Try to grasp all of the forms of suffering that are created by imagining possible scenarios that will likely never come to pass.

Can you isolate the idea or imagining that generates such activities as fretting, worrying, fearing, hurt feelings, jealousy, revenge, scheming, desiring, longing, craving, or dissatisfaction? What is imagined that generates the need to attain some ideal or try to find or have meaning? What conceptual-activities create inner turmoil and internal struggle and the sense of being personally flawed, produce the drive to keep constantly busy or distracted in order to avoid depression, and so on?

You may not see these concepts right away since so much is overlooked and taken for granted as the way things are. You have to dig into it. If you look, however, you can discover there is actually a mental activity taking place that is necessary to generate all of these things.

What thoughts have to occur to have self-worth, self-esteem, and a self-image? Think about it. Work on it. What do you imagine as a social world? Can you see how much of the social world is based on imagined stuff, conceptual stuff? What do you imagine people think about you? How much do you compare yourself with others or to social ideals? Inclusive and beyond social, what do you think will make you happy if you got it? What are you seeking that you don't have? All of these things are produced by or live in the world of *isn't*, and don't exist unless they're generated by you conceptually.

At this point your mind might be resisting and arguing with these assertions or perhaps just not understanding them. You may be trying to defend or excuse some of these mental activities, insisting they're necessary or perhaps unavoidable. Such reactions are based on misunderstanding what's being said or on a set and limited view of reality. Not to worry (a form of suffering); if you stick with it, all will become clear. Try not to focus on your inabilities or resistance but on the *facts*, and let the chips fall where they may.

You may be starting to get a sense of the magnitude of this conceptually dominated experience. It is all a world of idea-land, much of which is not necessary and none of which is objective; it is all made up. Among other things, it creates an unnecessary domain of suffering. You will probably not give it up altogether, but knowing what it is and how it exists, you can reduce and control it to a much greater degree and perhaps stay closer to or more frequently abide in the present and calm mind of a simpler creature.

How do you know if you are experiencing *is* or *isn't*? Ask this question: Is your experience solely about what is occurring in this moment presently and objectively? If so, it is about what is. If not, it is about what isn't. We're not talking about what is absolutely true or absolutely now. Here, we're concerned with simply what is experienced as life unfolding in present time.

Spending some time in an experience that is more like a simple uncomplicated animal, such as a rabbit, gives you a foundation or base from which to better see the influence of concepts on your experience and to better discern the more hidden conceptual aspects that masquerade as life experience when they are really only imagined. In order to produce such a "rabbit" experience, work to simply experience being a body for a period of time—perceiving life occurring in this moment without reference to an inner self and absent the plethora of ideas and imagination that tend to dominate a human experience.

Note that in "being a body" you don't think from within or look out from the inside, you simply perceive from the body out. Do this for a while and see how much this changes your experience. Don't worry about the practicality regarding your complex modern life; just do it to create a base and a contrast. There's more to get, but an experience of this simple objective-life creates the contrast needed to get it.

> *Do the difficult things while they are easy and*
> *do the big things while they are small.*
>
> Lao Tzu

CHAPTER FOUR

Mental Activities behind Most Forms of Suffering

BY BECOMING CONSCIOUS of how overlooked conceptualizations influence your experience, you will understand the impact these hidden activities have on you. There is a lot of *isn't* masquerading as *is*. It seems like they are inherent in the experience of real life, but they aren't. In order to dig into some of this, let's go over a bunch of common forms of suffering and consider what's behind them to see how they get constructed.

Again, for this to make a difference in your life experience, you need to get that all these concepts are something you are *doing* and not something that is just an aspect of your experience, as if imposed upon you against your will—which they are not. But you have to really grasp that in your experience. Once you experience that you are doing it and catch yourself doing it, you can stop doing it. If you don't stop generating those conceptualizations, you will continue to suffer the consequences for doing so.

To further clarify this domain of suffering-generating-conceptual-activities, let's look at a dozen rather commonplace examples that make up a lot of the unnecessary suffering we endure. Most people view such feeling-states as dissatisfaction, depression, and stress; being worthless,

flawed, disappointed, vulnerable, lonely, and alienated; having inner turmoil, shame, and grief, all as unwanted forms of suffering. Investigating
these subjects will provide the tools and direction to discover every
other form of suffering that might not be addressed here. You may not
find all of these particular forms of distress operating within you, or
maybe just on occasion, but it doesn't hurt to look into them all and
perhaps find something you haven't consciously noticed before.

DISSATISFACTION

We'll start with the prevalent malady of feeling dissatisfied with yourself and with your life, feeling like you are somehow incomplete and
in need of something more to be happy. Ever have that one? Consider:
What conceptual-activities have to occur for this to happen?

Although different concepts can contribute to this malady, there is
a theme—you are generating wanting something you don't have. Take
a look. You have to fixate on something in the domain of longing for
what is not occurring. If you stop that form of thinking, you end the
sense of being incomplete and dissatisfied. That simple.

Don't confuse this assertion with the old spiritual idea that craving or desire creates suffering. Although true, this is an unnecessary
bridge to cross. In this case, we are simply talking about those common
imaginations that unknowingly create dissatisfaction. You can't be dissatisfied with your life or yourself unless you imagine it should be some
other way. It is just not possible.

For example, say you live on a farm in the country, but you imagine that you need to be a Hollywood star in the big city in order to feel
fulfilled and satisfied with life. Yet you can imagine that a Hollywood
star might well feel too much stress and pressure and long for a quiet
life on a farm. So there is nothing inherent in your experience that
creates dissatisfaction. If you stop imagining some other life you think
is better, you won't be dissatisfied. Your life is your life, and it is fine
the way it is.

If you react to this reality by saying it would keep you down and not allow you to realize your full potential, this just isn't so. If you want to be a Hollywood star, then do the work—take acting classes and move to Hollywood! Comparing your imagination to your reality only creates suffering. Do something about it and it is now not something you are imagining but a reality you are living. If you don't do something, then shut the fuck up! Be happy with the life you are actually living, knowing it is what you are choosing.

Yet let's consider further. What is the ideation—the formation of ideas or concepts—behind going down the road of wanting what you don't have? You have to imagine that there is something better. Do you get that? You imagine there is something you don't have that you need in order to improve your experience. If this ideation is done away with then the conceptual-activity, and the resultant suffering because of it, won't occur.

In other words, stop imagining and dwelling on the idea and image that life should be some other way than it is, that there is something better that once attained would make you complete and satisfied. Doing so ends the sense of dissatisfaction. Do you find this hard to believe? Doesn't matter, it is actually true. This stuff doesn't exist on its own. Your mind has to create it.

It might sound like I am advocating for ignorance, to pretend or close your mind to other possibilities. Not at all. You can confront or imagine what you please, you can imagine what it might be like to be a Hollywood star if you like. The key is not to compare your current experience to it or think it is better or needed to make you whole and happy. Get it? The imagination itself doesn't create the suffering really, it is the comparison and better-than added to the imagination that does.

If you end this ideation and imagination, then you will not feel incomplete or dissatisfied with yourself or life. If you can't get this as a reality, contemplate and work on it until you can. Remember the rabbit; he should help you see what you are doing more clearly because he doesn't do any of this and doesn't suffer in that way.

It really does work that way, and it really is that simple. But it may not seem simple. You may run into excuses, justifications, and explanations that push the narrative that these mental activities are complex and needed. But justifications and excuses, clinging and defending, are just more of the same domain of activities that cause the suffering in the first place. Further, they make it seem like you have no choice, that life or circumstance is just that way. But this is a false conclusion.

To be clear, we are not talking about smoothing anything over, or applying a positive spin on things, or suppressing what's there in your mind. We are talking about stopping what's there! Ending that mental formulation. Watch your mind, see what it is you are doing. Stop thinking it and it doesn't exist. Suppression or overriding are serious mistakes. They only bury what you are doing. In this way, it is likely that what you're doing festers beneath the surface and just causes suffering in more indirect ways.

I know sometimes it can feel like a painful feeling is just there, that nothing has to happen to bring it about, such as a heartache that seems to reside in your chest unbidden. But the mind really doesn't work that way. If this is held to be the case, however, you'd have a hard time ridding yourself of it. Perhaps the only thing you could do is change your circumstances in an attempt to stimulate other feelings to override the painful one. Yet upon close inspection you should always be able to find what you are imagining, even if in the background, that produces this suffering.

Pining for a loved one who has left you can only occur if you dwell on them and their absence with the idea that their presence would end this suffering. But do you see the circular logic here? Of course, their presence would end the suffering; the suffering is about the "presence of their absence." Their presence ends that. But they are not there, they are absent for whatever reason. Is the heartache going to produce them or bring them back? One might think so. But it doesn't.

Can you go to them or go get them? If so, do it and no heartache continues. It disappears even prior to getting to them because now you are taking action and not just imagining. If this is not an option, then you can stop thinking about them being absent and simply live life as it is occurring. As with being dissatisfied, you have to imagine there is an experience better than what you are having in real life. In this way, you are relating to a conceptual-life that doesn't exist.

With this example, it isn't hard to see how the explanations might come flooding in, such as, "but it's real, they do exist, or did exist, and now they're gone; these are facts I can't do anything about and I must suffer them, there is no choice." Such mental activities might be very convincing and strong. Especially so because you believe them. Yet those "facts" have nothing to do with it.

You don't suffer the facts, you suffer wanting it to be otherwise. Stop your mind from wanting what you don't have and the suffering stops. If you can't (don't) do that, you will live with the consequences. If that is the case for you, I'd recommend looking into your own mind and finding what you are doing, and getting that you are doing it.

If you think you can't stop doing it and continue to suffer this activity, then go ahead and deliberately do it! Make it stronger and more pronounced if you like. Join with it and push yourself into doing it more. That way you can begin to get that it's something you're doing. If you can do it more, this suggests you are doing it in the first place. Once you experience doing it, then you can stop doing it.

DEPRESSION

Another rather common source of suffering is depression. Some people may get seriously or "clinically" depressed with a complex of causes possibly including physiological malfunction. But most people suffer some sort of depression, mild or major, from time to time that is solely caused by the mind. In such cases, what has to happen conceptually for depression to occur?

Obviously, you are undoubtedly seeing life as meaningless and as futile and hopeless. Why? You have created the ideation of imagining a negative future. You don't see a future where your needs are met. But when you're depressed it might look like you're depressed about your life now; what does the future have to do with it?

But think about it. If you're depressed because you've lost your job, your wife left you, and your dog died, these things have already taken place. These are the facts, aren't they? How can they not cause suffering? And how do they relate to the future?

Now, those people who characteristically get depressed probably don't find such obvious circumstances as the cause; much more background and unknown causes might be the norm. But the dynamic is the same. So, back to the scenario of losing your job, wife, and dog.

This might seem to be your current circumstance. But consider, if you had a better job in the wings, a more loving and compatible woman to relate to, and a cute new puppy, would you be depressed? Not likely. You might be a bit sad at your losses for a time, but the future looks positive and so you won't be depressed.

Certainly, such clear and dramatic causes won't be common, and much more obscure contributions are likely to be the cause of depression. But my assertion is that the mind is creating an assessment of life as it is that includes a bleak future, whether this is clear or not. In some way, you feel your well-being is not going to be taken care of, that your needs won't be met. If this is uncovered and replaced with a positive future, depression won't be an issue.

Such a positive future might look like being nurtured, cared for and loved, supported, being comfortable, or whatever. On the other hand, if you imagine that a future circumstance charged with making you "happy" is not possible, then depression can occur. Whether you realize it or not, you are in some way imagining a bleak and depressing future absent of what fulfills or sustains you.

Think about it. Excluding a real physiological malfunction, what else would cause depression? If you hold that it just occurs out of the blue, then I can't help you. You have to see it is something you are doing. If you create a positive future the depression will lift. I'm not saying that pretending some positive future is the best way to go, although it might well work, but finding and stopping the negative one is the key. The future is unknown, but this does not create depression.

Again, ever see a depressed rabbit? If there is such a thing it is extremely rare and undoubtedly not what we would experience as depression, nor caused by imagining—even if unconsciously and in the background—a negative future.

> *If you're going through hell,*
> *keep going.*
> WINSTON CHURCHILL

STRESS

Along similar lines, feeling stressed, worried, restless, paranoid, anxious, in despair, and whatnot are not uncommon for many people. We can also see that this domain of stress can easily have a physiological effect on the nervous system and the body. Physical maladies and disease can arise because of mental activities such as stress. So beyond suffering mentally, we should also acknowledge the physical damage that can result as well.

When it comes to stress and the like, what is being mentally generated that causes this form of suffering? For stress to occur, you have some conceptual-activity such as worrying or imagining feared or unwanted scenarios. Have you ever had such activities going on in your mind? Why would these activities occur? What foundation would make it possible and likely for them to arise?

The ideation behind them would be imagining something bad occurring. If you are worried, it is necessary to imagine bad things occurring and likely imagine specific scenarios of bad stuff arising. Do you see the links between stress and imagining bad things are going to happen? If you stop this worrying, or whatever, the stress dissipates.

I suspect many people will argue that they need to worry in order to be prepared to handle the possibility of bad things in case they occur. But one question: How often do you do this and how often has it proved worthwhile? Gaming out scenarios in order to work out possible responses can be done in a calm way that doesn't produce stress. But the vast amount of worry and stress is unproductive. When something bad does arise it most often is unexpected and so the worry scenario is not applicable. Also, most of the worry scenarios never come to pass and so fretting over something not real is a waste of time and energy and produces ill-effects in the body and the nervous system as well.

Of course, instead of worrying you could always take action if appropriate. If you have taken the needed action for safety or to manage whatever it is that you're stressing about, then nothing else can be done and worrying is useless and inappropriate. Independent of any rationalization for engaging in this mental activity, if you stop it, the distress it causes disappears.

Are you starting to see the dynamics involved? I am going through these quickly and briefly. I hope that brevity doesn't subtract from the profundity of what's being said and the power inherent in it. If you gloss over them, perhaps contemplate each until you grasp what's really being said and the reality behind them. This is not pop psychology.

WORTHLESSNESS

What about having low self-esteem or feeling unworthy? Ever have that one? What creates that kind of distress?

Obviously, you are generating some mental activity suggesting you are not good enough, that you are less than. This can't happen unless you compare yourself to others or to some ideals and see yourself as inferior and coming up short. Can you find the source ideation act behind this activity?

Being worthless only comes about through mental action, not observation. It just might seem like an observation, but what is actually observed doesn't diminish you. What is observed is a person or people are acting some way, or you are some way, and so on. Beyond such observations, however, you are assessing yourself in comparison to some imagined ideal suggesting you should be some way that you aren't. Without comparing yourself to other people or ideals you can't feel worthless or have low self-esteem. You wouldn't have critical self-judgments or the feelings that arise because of them. These are conceptual-activities, not observations.

If you have a hard time getting this, consider a rock. Is the rock worthless or less than? Less than what? It is exactly that rock. It can't be less than unless you compare it to another rock or some imagined rock, and it can't be worth anything or be worthless unless you assign some notion of worth. This requires a context in which some system of value is assigned to objects or rocks. It is the same with you. Unless you compare your assessment of you to some ideal and an imagined context of value, you can't be worthless or lack esteem. You are just you.

Once you get this, you can shift from holding what you previously saw as just true or occurring, to becoming conscious of the activity you are doing that causes this low self-esteem. Stop imagining an ideal and comparing yourself to it and you can't be worthless.

Sometimes people have deeply buried convictions about themselves that convince them they are worthless. But you can become conscious of this too and drop it. That usually requires contemplation. We will look into this domain a bit later in chapter 7, "Beneath the Surface."

Yet even without such introspection you can still stop the mental activities that generate these feelings, and they will stop. If you are wed to the idea of being worthless, however, it is likely to come back again because you will slip back into the mindset that produces it. Find that mindset and stop generating it.

Of course, people seem to have a rather simplistic view in their outlook about how this works, thinking the way to stop something negative is to imagine something positive. This is not what we are talking about here. You don't have to assert your worth. It is as irrelevant as being worthless. You simply have to stop generating and imagining ideals that show you as worthless in comparison. Being cannot be worthless; it just is. Only when you apply the activity of what isn't—by comparing, judging, imagining, and such—can the issue of worth arise. Stop doing that and you are freed from the domain of worth. You just are.

LONELINESS

Loneliness is one of the more core conditions for pretty much everybody. But it is most often buried under all of life's distractions—anything that keeps the mind busy and occupied. Yet there are occasions when we confront our loneliness and sometimes conditions press us into an experience of loneliness, especially during periods where others are absent from our lives.

I suspect most people have, at least from time to time, felt alone, isolated, perhaps unloved or discarded, or some such. For some people this is a major aspect of their self-experience, for others just an occasional thing. In either case, there is a deeper issue at play that involves our very sense of self.

What goes on so that one could feel lonely? You might desire but not have a close intimate relationship or partnership. This is a common form of loneliness. Yet even when there are people around, you can feel isolated and cut off. While being lonely your attention will very likely fall into your own private and isolated inner world. Such a focus tends to press you to contract into your sense of isolation even more. These are some of the dynamics involved in loneliness, but that doesn't answer the question: What mental activity causes loneliness?

Clearly, you are imagining that your happiness is dependent on some experience other than what you have and that this can only be produced by others and not you. In contrast, your current experience of living life by yourself is seen as lacking. You might also imagine others don't care about you or that something is wrong with you such that no one wants to be around you. Yet these last two points are explanations you might make up as to why you are alone but are still not the core cause and are really just rubbing salt in the wound, so to speak.

The foundation ideation that sets the stage for such suffering stems from the fact that you live in a private inner world that only you experience and this is held as the place where you reside. But no one else can ever also reside in this "place." So you will always be alone there and the only avenue to connect with another private inner world is through communication. Here you might be able to develop a sense of connection. But this can't be done without others, and so you feel you need others, and often a special other, in order to be intimately connected.

When this isn't happening, you can easily feel alone, isolated, and lonely. Acknowledging that such a deep connection with another is usually rather rare means most of the time you live on an island of separation. With or without people, to avoid suffering loneliness you probably feel the need to be distracted, to have something fill your mind and experience so you don't have to face the deep loneliness that you feel just being a self.

Clearly you aren't OK with being alone. You aren't OK with merely "being," and you need some form of distraction from this condition. It seems that your mere existence as a being is incomplete and you need the imagined "promise" that someone or others can somehow complete your experience. These ideations are foundational to this lonely form of suffering.

> The fundamental delusion of humanity is to suppose that
> I am here and you are out there.
>
> YASUTANI ROSHI

Did you follow that? Let's go over it again. The core concept is that you aren't OK just being you and you need others to complete you in order to make you happy. Since you live in an existentially isolated private inner-self world the only avenue to connect to another is through communication. And you need others for that. So, in this way, living as an incomplete self tends to cause loneliness.

What might also be true, beyond this basic human condition, is that you personally might have an existential assumption that you are unlovable or not worth being loved or accepted as you are, which isn't going to help matters. To understand more about existential assumptions—since some of these ideations might be founded on them—see chapter 22 in *The Book of Not Knowing*, or attend relevant workshops. It can be a tricky domain to understand, so work needs to be done. The bottom line is that they are simply aspects of what you are doing with your mind. They tend to be unconscious and overlooked, but becoming conscious of them allows you to stop doing them.

Independent of freedom from some existential assumption, your experience of loneliness requires imagining another possible world that you don't have. I know it might seem like you have no choice about it, as if it is just a fact of circumstance—and what makes it even worse, this notion is supported by the culture in which you live. Yet try to grasp where that "fact" lives. It lives solely in your imagination and what you say this condition means to you. You are alone and you imagine not being alone would be a more satisfying experience.

In contrast to an imagined circumstance, you see your current experience as negative and unacceptable. You desire or long for something that you don't have (sound familiar?). Again, you assess that you, by yourself, are not good enough, are not complete without someone else to validate you. Your self-experience is felt to be lacking and incomplete. Therefore, you judge your current "imagined" experience as negative and painful.

Why do I say current "imagined" experience? Certainly, if it is your experience you aren't imagining it but experiencing it, right? Actually, not really. What you currently experience is your body and what you perceive as occurring both physically and conceptually. But, unless you just stubbed your toe or something, there is no pain or suffering in this experience. And with or without pain, there is no loneliness there. The loneliness is added through imagining comparisons as mentioned above, and so what is currently experienced is given a negative meaning. This is added and it is imagined. Stop imagining this added layer to your experience and it doesn't exist. And the suffering doesn't arise.

Again, I acknowledge that since we are social animals and have also developed an overactive ability to imagine all sorts of stuff, this change of mind could seem difficult. I know for the vast majority of people that it is a difficult challenge to overcome because we think such experiences as loneliness are inevitable, a fact that we must suffer. So it is easy to overlook the power we have to simply not compare what is factually occurring with this imagined experience that is not occurring.

But, hard as it is to accept, a deep loneliness tends to be a core experience for most humans even when it is overridden with distractions. When your attention is being filled with active life activities you won't notice the loneliness aspect, nor necessarily should you. But it is still a dynamic that should be dealt with. It will come around to bite you in the ass at some point, especially as you get older.

It is useful to work on "completing" yourself—grasping you are already complete and whole and that your experience is all that is needed no matter what it is. This goes a long way toward ending this malady. (We will go into this more in the section "Being Complete" on page 116.) J. Krishnamurti speaks to this malady and suggests it is deeper than most of us think:

Try being alone, without any form of distraction, and you will see how quickly you want to get away from yourself and forget what you are. That is why this enormous structure of professional amusement . . . is so prominent a part of what we call civilization. If you observe, you will see that people the world over are becoming more and more distracted, increasingly sophisticated and worldly. . . . Because we are inwardly empty, dull, mediocre, we use our relationships and our social reforms as a means of escaping ourselves. I wonder if you have noticed how lonely most people are. And to escape from loneliness we run to temples, churches, or mosques, we dress up and attend social functions, read, and so on. . . .

If you inquire a little into boredom you will find that the cause of it is loneliness. It is in order to escape from loneliness that we want to be together, we want to be entertained, to have distractions of every kind, gurus, religious ceremonies, prayers, or the latest novel. Being inwardly lonely we become mere spectators in life; and we can be the players only when we understand loneliness and go beyond it.

. . . because beyond it lies the real treasure.

DISAPPOINTMENT

It isn't unusual for us to be disappointed from time to time. Sometimes our disappointment can be deep and dramatic and at other times it can be a rather minor glitch. So again, our first question is how is it possible to be disappointed?

Obviously, we can't be disappointed with what is or what happens unless we have expectations it should be otherwise. As with so many of these forms of suffering, we must imagine we need or want something that is not present or not occurring. When we create this contrast, we find our current experience is not what we expected or wanted it to be and so are disappointed.

The rather simple ideation behind this possibility would center around generating notions about the future, imagining how things are going to turn out or should turn out. Perhaps this extends to ideals or fantasies we think should be the case, which might be the cause of deeper types of disappointment. Yet we can't be disappointed with a fantasy that simply remains a fantasy. We have to think it is real and should take place in real life. When it doesn't, we are upset and feel let down by reality.

Of course, you can stop this kind of mental activity. Stop imagining life should be some way that it isn't or expect it should be and you're not disappointed. You are likely to still engage in such mental activity and thus be disappointed sometimes, but you can also recognize quickly what you've done and shift to what is rather than remain focused on and bemoaning what isn't.

By now we are starting to see a pattern to the conceptual-activities we generate and the suffering caused by generating them. We also see the solution—stop doing it. This applies to all of these forms of suffering. But let's continue with more examples to help bring it home to a greater degree.

FLAWED

It's not uncommon for people to suffer a feeling of being flawed, imperfect, somehow broken, perhaps inauthentic or fake, and the like. Some people have this experience as common and up front; many have such feelings but keep them buried or purposely ignored and suppressed. But most people have some form of this as a part of their self-experience. Can you find something in this domain for you?

In the case of being flawed or inadequate, what mental conceptions produce this kind of suffering? Possible contributing conceptual-activities could be doubting yourself, being self-critical, and having negative self-judgments. Ever encounter any of this kind of mental consternation? But these activities are just the tip of the iceberg.

Many of these forms of suffering can have similar components in their makeup, and the consequences for having them may also be similar. In this case, again, you imagine that you need something that isn't true for you, having expectations that aren't what you experience. In order for this to happen you will be relating to some "ideal" regarding what or how you should be and find yourself seriously lacking.

Again, what ideation would generate such mental activities? The foundation notion is that there is some perfect or ideal experience that should be the case for you and for your life or your experience. Can you see that not only is this not real, but it is a damaging ideation to create? Most people can't. They look at ideals as hope for their lives, the attainment of which will fix the personal maladies they experience as their self-condition or the condition of their lives. But not only is this false, it creates the very suffering they were trying to avoid.

Behind the creation of such an ideal is the ideation of assuming that you are existentially broken and need to be fixed or that you are inherently flawed as a person and need to be mended or perfected. This is what the ideal is based upon—why it exists. Seems a bit circular, doesn't it? But the domain of your experience where this usually buried existential self-assumption lives is deeper, so to speak, than the thoughts that arise because of it. It is held as simply true of you and your life will be based upon it—even though you might spend your time endlessly resisting, denying, covering up, or compensating for it.

For example, let's say I have an overlooked ideal that I should be the "perfect" person and have background images of what that would look like. Of course, this is accompanied by the notion that if accomplished I would then finally be whole and complete and so live happily-ever-after. From attaining this ideal I imagine that life will be as it should be and all my distress and problems will disappear.

Intellectually we might understand this isn't going to happen, that realistically it's not a grounded possibility. But that doesn't stop us from having it, especially in the background where it doesn't show up on the surface for what it is. What shows in your experience is instead the dissatisfaction and disappointment in the person that you are and the life that you have. Behind this form of suffering is the ideation that you should attain some ideal, thinking this will resolve your suffering.

I have explained in detail elsewhere that such resolution can't happen because the effort to attain something to "complete" you is aimed in the wrong direction. Resolution of whatever is experienced as wrong, broken, or inadequate about you can only be had by you from within, not from without. Generating ideals as something that should be, but aren't, only creates suffering within your current experience.

If you can't see that what you are doing with your mind is the cause of the experience you have, then you can't stop doing it. On the other hand, whether or not you deeply grasp the assumptions you live within that produce such ideals, if you simply stop having the ideals and stop imagining that what *isn't* (an ideal you) should replace what is, the suffering dissolves. Stop being self-critical or thinking you are broken or flawed in some way and, instead, grasp that you are already whole and complete the way you are, and all the suffering that arises from picking at that scab will disappear.

VULNERABLE

Have you ever had a sense of vulnerability, helplessness, or powerlessness? Perhaps these resulted in distress, fear, or feeling incapable, and maybe extended to generating such states as hopelessness, lethargy, procrastination, withdrawal, or timidity, or perhaps defiance, resistance, defensiveness, and so on. Ever experience anything in this domain? Probably everyone has. You may have successfully navigated your way out of this sense, but the feelings still arise from time to time, and for some people they are frequent.

In reality, vulnerability is a fact. You can be hurt, damaged, and you will die. In the face of death, you are literally powerless to prevent it. But, again, we aren't considering physical forms of suffering. The vulnerability we are looking at here is the product of mental-emotional imagination. Our sense of vulnerability or helplessness applies to our egos and our emotional selves. We *feel* vulnerable and suffer this experience. Regardless of the circumstance that seems to contribute to this feeling, what is necessary in order for it to occur?

Obviously, you need to generate the idea that you have no control over some aspect of life and so are helpless to successfully resolve or manage life or circumstances. When it comes to a physical circumstance that is out of your control, you might feel vulnerable. Any "facts" in this matter are rather irrelevant. For example, you may hear someone say something or watch them behave in some way. These might be facts of circumstance. But feeling vulnerable is another matter.

In a physical scenario, you are only vulnerable if it can cause physical damage. But adding a feeling of helplessness even to this physical assessment is a form of suffering. In this consideration, however, vulnerability relates more to subjective concerns as are found in human relations—someone says something or behaves in some way—and these "facts" aren't what create the feeling of vulnerability, but instead mind makes it so.

This is likely based upon an ideation of imagining that others have power over your experience, that they can determine what you experience and are doing so in a way that is not in your best interest. Therefore, you imagine that your life can't work out for you as you would like—or something along those lines. Yet *you* have to give them the power to control you with their words or behavior. You may have no control over their behavior but you do have a choice over how you relate to it and how it affects you. Stop generating this mind activity and the suffering goes away. You can only feel vulnerable if you make it that way. It might be automatic, and you might be strongly programmed to do it, but if you stop doing it, this "malady" won't persist.

That doesn't necessarily mean that you suddenly feel invulnerable or you become excited and energetic about your newfound superpowers. Maybe that happens, but it really depends on what else comes to mind. Yet it does mean that wallowing in the despair of helplessness or hopelessness is no longer occurring. Whatever else arises is up to you. Of course, this is the case for all of these forms of suffering. Don't think that because something stops, the opposite is then the case. It only means that that something stopped.

Outside of actually being physically damaged, what's going to happen because you have an emotional feeling of vulnerability? Are you going to die or be physically damaged? No. So what are you going to lose or suffer? Humiliation? Embarrassment? Someone taking advantage of you against your will? Hurt your feelings? Be exposed in some way? Damage your pride or dignity? Be disturbed by someone saying something bad about you? Sure, whatever.

None of this can occur, however, without your contribution. It can't occur unless you are a partner in it. You have to give them power over you and so create in your mind that you are vulnerable. You have to think that what someone says or does somehow damages you, otherwise it can't happen. Stop generating these concepts; allow whatever is true to be the case and you aren't vulnerable.

I know this is unusual and may seem impossible, but it's not. It's just not something we have been taught to do, and because we are strongly attached to our social concerns we might find it difficult to let go of those concerns. On the other hand, if we let go of such concerns or don't mentally give others power to affect us in this way, we won't suffer this outcome.

One very powerful perspective to have in this and many other forms of discomfort begins by noticing that you allow others' behavior to affect you emotionally. Certainly, this is a knee-jerk reaction and disposition. Notice that you are "at the effect" of—meaning are affected by, or that your experience reacts to—everything you perceive. Clearly this applies to others. When they say something or behave some way, you automatically change your experience in relation to what's there. Within this dynamic, vulnerability can be created, but as you can see, this dynamic also applies to so much more.

A powerful change in perspective is to see what others do as how it affects them, not as how it affects you. What they say and do is a reflection of their experience and choices. Don't make it about you. You can always reflect on their communication and ask if there is any truth to it regarding yourself, but that is different from being at the effect of it. For example, if someone is angry at you, you see the anger as affecting them, creating suffering for them, not how it affects you. Instead of feeling reactive to their anger, you might feel sorry for them choosing to suffer that experience. Can you grasp this shift? See what others do as *how it affects them, not how it affects you.* Obviously, it would take training because you've been programmed to see it the other way. But I recommend that you file this away and use it as much as you can.

See what others do as how it affects them, not how it affects you.

ALIENATION

It is not uncommon for people to justify and excuse their behavior and mental activities. It is a frequent almost unconscious act for most people. This not only creates a particular mindset, it also has consequences that most often go overlooked because the connection isn't made between action and consequence. This reflexive reaction to your behavior—that you see as embarrassing, unacceptable, selfish, or what have you—tends to elicit excuses and justifications, attempting to modify or eliminate blowback for such acts.

This tendency could be accompanied by other perspectives. You might feel like an inherent fuck-up and so constantly excuse and justify your missteps or ineffective or inappropriate actions. On the other hand, you could feel self-important and special, holding yourself—often without thinking—as being right no matter what your viewpoint or behavior is. No matter the perspective, your automatic tendency to defend yourself in this way cuts off any genuine level of feedback and learning regarding your habitual thinking and behavior patterns.

Often overlooked is that this activity creates consequences that are forms of suffering. Such defensive actions increase your sense of isolation and boost the tendency to be insensitive by having diminished empathy. It cuts off feedback about yourself, alienates others, and promotes an unconscious tendency toward arrogance. In a social context, these will all produce forms of suffering. And yet the fact of the suffering is often not known for what it is because of the defensive nature of this behavior and the obvious focus on oneself to the exclusion of facts or other viewpoints. Therefore, it is unlikely to be recognized as the source of one's unhappy circumstance—which is also likely to be justified and excused. Instead, you will tend to blame others, circumstance, or "life" for your unhappiness.

What ideations could source this behavior, perspective, and consequence? This is a little trickier to unearth than some, because the link to how it unfolds into suffering is rather convoluted. As a foundation, again, we think we reside in a private inner world that no one else really knows about and assume that this world and its activities are very important to our self-survival. We also think that since no one else knows what goes on in there, whatever we do has no consequences. Wrong again.

We empower this inner-self world as the arbiter of what is right and wrong and assume it is never wrong itself. From here it isn't a huge leap to assume that whatever one thinks or does needs defending because these activities are seen as expressions of "ourselves" and our existence is tied to our expressions and viewpoint, so we will be slow to see them as mistaken or in error. As a matter of fact, for reasons requiring too much time to fully address here, the activities that go on within one's inner world, or mind, are most often inaccurate as they are not based on a clear and unbiased view of whatever is true in whatever is being considered. So the errors here are abundant but they are not at all seen that way due to this knee-jerk defensive dynamic.

An assumption that often accompanies this disposition is that one's self is more important than others. Obviously for each of us this is true, since we see ourselves as the only essential ingredient necessary for existence. Also, central to this suffering may be seeing social interactions and feedback as in conflict with self-interests. Such an assumption serves to divide us from the interests and experience of others and this has consequences. It tends to prevent us from recognizing the ineffectiveness or errors in our own thinking and behavior because our focus is on defending them.

By engaging in defensive behaviors in both speech and mind and by excusing and justifying our own self-behavior, unnecessary suffering occurs as a consequence. Can you see these links? Most people can't, especially if they are the ones being defensive. Look into this alienating form of suffering and see if you can find anything in that domain for you, and if so, then see if you can trace how this mental disposition and activity create overlooked forms of suffering.

∽

There, but for the grace of god, go I.

INNER TURMOIL

Almost everyone judges themselves, others, and life, at least from time to time and very often negatively. What may be overlooked in this action is that being critical of self, others, or circumstance leads to an inner turmoil as you struggle to manage the unacceptable feelings caused by it. This turmoil might be taken for granted as just a part of life or inflicted on you by life. After all, the circumstance seems to force the judgment because it is seen that way, as good or bad. But consider, in contrast to having a calm, easy, and open internal experience—absent of turmoil—can you see this is actually a form of suffering you might live with?

Obviously, inner turmoil can be generated by all sorts of activities—certainly worry, longing, stress, and other mental activities will create such disturbance. But in this consideration, we are looking at a kind of inner struggle that isn't obvious and tends to be overlooked. This disturbance is based on something we do, but we rarely connect the dots that these actions have consequences that lead to a form of suffering.

What ideation occurs such that we would naturally go down the road of criticism? We see that we assess everything in relation to ourselves, we assess the negative or positive effect it has on us. "What does it mean to *me*, how does it affect *me*?" These are knee-jerk reactions to anything encountered but seem like they are mere perceptions. From these apparent perceptions, we form a judgment regarding what's there, is it good or bad, and so on. This dynamic creates an experience that is then circumstantially derived.

What do I mean by circumstantially derived? It means that your experience is dependent on and appears caused by whatever circumstance is perceived. Since you are at the effect of whatever is perceived, this then creates the experience that you have. That makes it "circumstantially derived."

A negative judgment produces a negative reaction and it will seem as if you have no choice. The reaction produced by judging others or life negatively will appear as if caused by the others or life, even though the judgments are of your own making. If the judgments are about other than you, then they are seen as the cause of your experience and even the cause of your judgments. If you're judging yourself, then your failings are seen as caused by you.

Having our experience be circumstantially derived is not at all uncommon. It is the norm and true for almost everyone. In this case, however, the thing we are trying to see is the specific role negative judgments have in causing distress. If we can get some space from relating everything to ourselves, we find an opportunity available to us that otherwise wouldn't exist.

Not relating everything to yourself may be difficult, since such mental activity is engrained in your perceptions as an automatic function. But it is also unnecessary to do it for everything in order to make headway ending this form of suffering. Although the activity of judging tends to be automatic, with a little attention you can notice you are doing it and can stop doing it. Even without giving up all judging, you can at least discover the judgments of yourself and others or life that create most of your turmoil and stop those mental activities.

Have you ever considered or encountered examples of the archetypical wise old person—rare as it is? They are unusual because they're slow to judge and react the way most of us do. They have learned over a lifetime that most of the stuff we react to isn't worth the grief and is often just a paper tiger. So they calmly meet the situation with equanimity and counsel patience. We might learn a lesson from them. One way to approach this dilemma is to accept things as is, to let them be the way they are without resistance or reacting to what's perceived. This creates the space to stop the automatic judgments and so the consequences for doing so.

Again, this doesn't necessarily provide an opposite experience. It simply frees you of that activity. If you judge yourself negatively, stopping that doesn't give you a positive experience. It gives you an experience of you without that judgment and perhaps without judgment altogether. This is an important distinction because if you are shooting for the opposite, trying to impose a positive judgment, you are still caught in the same activity, just with different content. So you won't really understand or get free of this activity. Instead, it will turn into trying to override your real assessment by pretending something positive is true instead.

Suspending your judgments and accepting what is *as is*, is not necessarily done for others, it is done for you because you realize it causes suffering. Eliminating the activity of judging is not about submitting to what is assessed as in need of correction; such correction can be done without reacting to negative judgments—which don't actually change anything, they just cause distress. Taking action, on the other hand, isn't about mental activity, it is about action—we will go into this distinction a great deal in the next chapter. The essential point is you don't stop judging to be a "good" person or to benefit others, you do it because it lifts the inner turmoil caused by it.

Certainly, we have covered enough examples so far to get a handle on the dynamics that cause unnecessary suffering. All other forms of suffering can now be discovered by following the same pattern of investigation we've seen in what we've already covered:

- Isolate the form of suffering you are enduring.
- Discover what concept or mental activity you engage that generates that form of suffering.
- Go deeper to discover what ideations you have created that make such mental activity seem necessary.
- Then eliminate both ideation and mental activity and the suffering disappears.

But let me briefly touch on two more forms of suffering, a bit different from the others, just to push the envelope a bit.

SHAME

Continuing in the same vein, people sometimes suffer such feelings as shame, guilt, and embarrassment. Clearly, we hold these experiences as forms of suffering. What happens in our minds when we produce such feelings? We imagine—or what we might call assess—that our behavior, and perhaps very person, is socially unacceptable. It seems the ideation is viewing yourself or your behavior as wrong in the eyes of others.

Again, if this is commonplace for you, the ideation will be a core self-assumption, so it might take some contemplation on your part to unearth its reality. Yet you can interrupt this impulse by not imagining, not creating the idea, that you are unacceptable. If you are pursuing psychopathic or antisocial pathology then perhaps such consequences are appropriate to help orient you into acceptable behavior. Yet, if you are simply neurotic or programmed with self-doubt, not engaging in this activity can free you from unnecessary suffering. Again, accepting yourself as you are lifts this form of distress.

What's also true is these are merely feelings, unwanted experiences. You can shift your disposition to embracing the feeling instead of resisting it. If you fully allow it to be, not fighting the feeling, it becomes something like a rush, an interesting and perhaps unusual experience. This shift in your disposition reduces and perhaps eliminates the suffering aspect of these experiences.

GRIEF

Of course, most people suffer such emotions as grief, sadness, sorrow, and so on. If these are a repeated pattern or occur more than rarely, you might want to ask what scenarios of personal hurt are you entertaining? There has to be something you imagine to be true that generates such reactions in you. Stop imagining those scenarios and the reactions don't occur. If you stop dwelling on what you've lost or stop holding that past circumstances or others have damaged or threatened you in some way, you will short-circuit these forms of suffering.

In some cases when you've experienced loss, grief might be appropriate for a time, allowing your mind to adjust to this loss. But if it goes on for a long time, it seems the healing function isn't working and something else is at play that isn't healthy. As with all of these forms of distress, stop doing any of the parts of the process that are necessary to create that experience and those forms of suffering won't continue to arise.

BRINGING IT HOME

These examples address some of the most common forms of suffering for humans. If you have forms of suffering not found here, you can use the same investigative technique and find the ideation and mental activity you are generating that causes that suffering—just follow the same basic patterns as above.

Again, I am not talking about physical pain, such as breaking a leg or having a heart attack. This form of suffering is biological in nature and not something you are doing conceptually. For sure, you can and usually do add a great deal of mental-emotional suffering on top of the physical, and when you don't do that the "suffering" is far less. Yet for most people significant physical pain is infrequent—as to those for whom it's frequent, I feel for them. But for most of us physical pain is not the predominant or constant form of suffering, but mental-emotional pain is.

As I indicated earlier, these forms of suffering aren't limited to those clearly acknowledged overwhelming emotional pains, such as heartbreak or losing a loved one, or the stressful traumatic emotional trials and tribulations one might undergo. They are also found in overlooked aspects we tend to hold as just the way life is—feeling incomplete, being dissatisfied with life, feeling less than or worthless, being depressed, feeling meaningless, inauthentic, lonely, bored, and so on. These are all unnecessary. They are something we are doing but likely don't know we are doing and instead we feel they are just inflicted upon us. They aren't. Stop doing what causes them and they can't occur.

But you still might ask, how do I do that? Well, take a moment and do the following exercise.

Mind Exercise

Right now, have a thought, any thought.
OK, now stop having that thought.

Now, imagine something.
Great, stop imagining it.

Now, picture the future turning out some way in particular.
Just make something up.
Fine, now stop imagining that future scenario.

Now, have a negative judgment about yourself.
Good, now stop judging yourself.

Terrific. Imagine a better life than what you have.
OK, stop imagining that.

Are you getting the picture? This is something you can and do engage in. It is the same with all those thoughts and imaginings that produce suffering. You might think you have reasons demanding that you think them, but really those only exist because you think they exist—that they are necessary and real. Stop thinking you have to think them and you don't have to think them. Just as you controlled your mind in the exercise above, stop the conceptual-activities you're doing that generate suffering and the consequences that result from those activities will also stop.

I don't want to give the impression that stopping thoughts that seem like an imperative for you will seem easy. The actual ability to do it is as easy as doing it, but the drive to keep the thought going can be quite strong and you may find no desire to drop it, thinking that this concept is something you need to have. Yet this very desire is also a thought you can drop, as is the need.

The only reason you cling so desperately to a thought that causes suffering is because you believe it is a necessary part of your self-survival. Separating your self-concerns from your ability to control your mind helps bridge this chasm between self-drives and your ability to stop a thought. As I heard in a song once: "don't let the sound of your own wheels drive you crazy."* Sound advice.

To ground this further, let's take a clear example of a solid form of suffering and see what thoughts create it. Fear is obviously seen as suffering, but most people think it is a necessary experience they can't avoid when something scary arises. What's overlooked here, however, is the scary thing hasn't actually arisen—only the thought of it has. Most people have a hard time grasping this difference. Fear is always only about the future. You are afraid something unwanted *might* happen. If it *is* happening you aren't afraid, you are in some sort of pain.

Again, to see this more clearly, set aside concern for your safety and survival. Now notice that when you are afraid you are imagining an unwanted experience might come about. If you stop imagining this, no fear can arise. Can you get that?

Try it out with something rather benign—like fearing a meteor might fall on your head or that a monster is going to break down your door to attack you. Since in this moment you know you are just making those up and the likelihood they will occur right now is slim, you have an easier time separating out your concerns from your ability to not

---

*"Take It Easy," written by Jackson Browne and Glenn Frey, was the Eagles' first single.

have such thoughts. So have the thought, as best you can, until you get nervous or afraid.

Now, stop imagining that thought. You see? The fear goes away. It actually can't happen because the fear is dependent on the imagination of a future scenario. Can you make the distinction between your ability to generate or not generate that scenario and the self-concerns that might push you to generate it?

Certainly, you might have a much harder time doing this when a tiger is coming at you. It is possible, but because your physical survival is at stake you may well opt to use the fear to propel you up a tree. To be clear, you don't actually need the fear to motivate you, you only need to recognize the danger and take action. At the time, however, you'll likely consider that bringing up this fact is just splitting hairs. Can you see the difference between the ability and self-survival concerns?

This example gives you a better sense of where you have to go within your mind to end suffering. When it comes to all your unnecessary suffering, most of it is far easier than ending such impending fear, but the dynamic is the same. Think about it. We've touched on many examples and solutions for ending suffering, and you've likely come up with more when you've looked into your own personal challenges. You can see that these are probably not as hard as eliminating the fear of the presence of a charging tiger. And again, physical suffering isn't our concern here—although in reality you will only physically suffer when the tiger gets you, not when you are afraid of him doing so. But you may not appreciate this distinction at the time.

For most social suffering, remember the axiom: *see what others do and say as how it affects them, not how it affects you*. This is gold. But it's likely to fall into disuse because your focus will automatically be on you and this will engender relating what's encountered to how it affects you. But you can change that, and the more you do, the easier access you'll have to this shift and the more likely it is to happen.

The point is, to be successful with this work, you need to experience what you are doing "within your mind" that creates suffering.

You have to "find" the place where it actually happens before you can change it. Another thing you need to do is experientially make a distinction between the mental activities that cause suffering and those that don't—I will address this distinction in the next chapter.

> *Happiness is not a reward—it is a consequence.*
> *Suffering is not a punishment—it is a result.*
> ROBERT GREEN INGERSOLL

CHAPTER FIVE

Transforming the Mind to End Suffering

CONCEPTUAL-ACTION VERSUS CONCEPTUAL-ACTIVITY

Since we are conceptual creatures, we're not going to give up all concepts, nor should we. But there are concepts that create suffering and those that don't and some that even enhance life. Therefore, we need to make a distinction between these two domains of conceptualizations.

To say it in another way, one thought you have will cause suffering and another won't. What is the difference between these two thoughts? You need to know this in order to proceed successfully and start doing the work of ending unnecessary suffering.

For clarity, I invented two terms to label each of these domains. The domain of mind that causes suffering of various kinds I'm calling "conceptual-activity." Mind that is taking action, even though it's conceptual in nature, but is still related to real life and can be life enhancing, I'm calling "conceptual-action."

Conceptual-activities aren't related to real life as it is occurring in present time. Activities in this domain are generating fantasies, imagination, beliefs, assumptions, comparisons, desires, ideals, expectations, and the like. Generally, those activities occur without any intent to make anything conceived become objectively real, but this is overlooked. Instead, this domain is just *thought* to be true or needed, but it is neither.

Conceptual-activity is rather like mental masturbation. It is not about taking action that makes a difference in real life—even though it appears most people think it does. Certainly it influences your experience and in this way affects your life because it influences your decisions and your interpretations of events. But all of that is unnecessary, although very common and usually automatic. Of course, such influence creates a great deal of suffering. What isn't noticed, however, is that it is all conceptual and is not related to what is objectively so—therefore it is unnecessary and not inherently real. It is only mental activity, figments of mind and imagination, not action.

Conceptual-action, on the other hand, is action. It does not cause suffering, even though it is conceptual. It is mental action applied to real life, or life as it's lived not life as it's imagined. The content of the domain of conceptual-action includes such acts as intent, commitment, contemplation, planning real-life activities, problem-solving, inventing something like a feeling-image to help you accomplish a skill in life, creative imagination not bound to fantasy, effective or powerful principles to adopt that empower life, and so on. Conceptual-actions do not cause suffering.

Again, as best you can, imagine the mind of a rabbit. What is *not* going on for the rabbit? Certainly, even if they have a modicum of conceptual ability, it is always present and directed to life as it's lived. They have no conceptual-activity, although they may have some conceptual-action. This contrast helps you see all the unnecessary conceptual stuff humans add to life. Grasp that all that stuff is obviously not necessary for life to occur or to occur successfully and happily—just remember the rabbit.

To help ground this distinction, so we can better choose action rather than activity, let's look at how concept can be used to enhance real life. To reiterate, concept lives in a world of *isn't*, meaning it isn't objective or necessary. It is activity that occurs only as a figment of mind. *Is*, on the other hand, is real. It is objective biological life as it is occurring. If the distinction between conceptual-activity versus conceptual-action isn't experientially clear yet, it should become clear in the next section. So how can we make our *isn't* serve and apply to what *is*?

> *It always seems impossible until it's done.*
> NELSON MANDELA

ALIGNING WHAT ISN'T WITH WHAT IS

Of course, as a human living in a sophisticated modern culture that requires the use of concepts to manage life, we will not let go of all concept. Yet starting from a clear and simple experience of merely "being"—like our rabbit example—we can better consider what domains of concept might be useful to retain and in what forms they can be brought to align with and support what is, without all the unnecessary activities that create suffering and dissatisfaction.

As mentioned, conceptual-action by itself doesn't generate suffering. When we can experience what this domain is—and know why it doesn't create suffering—we are better equipped to use conceptualization powerfully to support life rather than create distress.

There are conceptual-actions that compel *isn't* to align with *is*. For example, commitment, grounded realistic planning, creating states that serve a life function in present time, and adopting certain principles. Why do these conceptual-actions or principles bring *isn't* into *is*? Let's take a look.

Again, conceptual-activity is all that lame stuff that creates suffering or is just a useless waste of mental energy that goes nowhere. A great deal of our habitual mental movements are conceptual-activities. Recall all of the ideations and mental activities we went through in the previous chapter that cause suffering and you have many examples of conceptual-activity. Notice that besides causing suffering, conceptual-activities occur detached from real life and are really just figments of mind bouncing around inside your head. It is very commonplace and should not be hard to find. But knowing which is activity and which is action might take some more work.

As I've mentioned, conceptual-actions are actions, not just thoughts about action. They are done now about now and support real-life activities. The main goal is that whatever concept we have, regardless of the form, it is itself an action or leads to action of some kind.

For example, intent is conceptual-action. But to be clear, there's often confusion between desire and intention. Intention isn't the desire for something that may or may not happen. It is the impulse that makes something happen. Desire, on the other hand, is simply musing about wanting something. Usually we use these terms interchangeably, and so have no clear lines to make them distinct. But for our work here we need them to be distinct because we are making a distinction between activity and action.

Intent is about the action, not the mental activity of desire without action. When we hold it that way we can see the difference. When you desire something, you are merely imagining and pining for something conceptually. This is not an action—it is a conceptual-activity and it often leads to suffering. It is also an overlooked form of suffering itself.

Instead, when you intend to do something or obtain something, this is an action because the impulse for action will follow on the heels of this intent. If it doesn't, it's not intent. There may be something of "wanting" inherent in the impulse of intent, but the distinction here is that desire is just wanting without action and intent is wanting inseparable from action. Do you see how intent then relates to real life?

It is the same for conceptual-actions like commitment. Committing yourself to a real-life goal or action is applying concept to life. This act is not responsible for suffering. Commitment demands that we give some degree of our life energies to realizing a goal. This requires taking action in present time—as is appropriate to stay on track with the process of attempting to realize our objective.

For example, say I want more trees growing on the mountain. So the moment I commit to that, I take action. In this case, what is involved in growing a tree? First, I have to get a seed to germinate and start the tree growing. So I go get seeds and start them growing in my hothouse. My commitment is to the trees maturing on the mountain, so until the young trees are ready to plant I do nothing toward this commitment except care for the baby trees. When they are ready, I walk them up the mountain and plant them.

The point is, commitment devotes the necessary life actions to accomplish a task, and at certain times that may be nothing. Intent, on the other hand, means I take the action intended now. The very nature of committing to something occurs in present time—whether appropriate action is taken immediately or later as needed. This means commitment creates action, pushing us toward what is, not what isn't. Contrast this to fantasy, wishful thinking, desire, ideals, comparisons, and so on, and you can see that commitment attaches life to the present and not merely to idea-land.

In the same way, grounded and realistic planning demands a sober understanding of logistics and how things actually work, as well as the intention to make such plans real. You can see that you can't make anything real unless it shows up in present time. Thus, this domain of planning is founded on merging what's planned with what is, until it happens. This demands you take action in each part of the planned process as it unfolds—again, pushing you to relate to *is* not *isn't*.

We see that contemplation—setting out to become conscious of what's true about the nature of something—always occurs in present time. One reason this is true is because what is—ergo what *is true*— exists only in present time. Contemplation is about pursuing what's true about existence, and existence always and only exists now.

Therefore, contemplation, no matter what is done or how it is done—if the intent is to honestly grasp what's true—will always drive us toward this moment and real life. Contemplation doesn't cause suffering. We might suffer frustration and so on while trying to contemplate but those are generated by mental activities regarding our inability to make a breakthrough, not the action of contemplation itself. Of course, we could possibly suffer a sore ass if we choose to sit for long periods in our contemplating efforts, but again, that is physical discomfort and out of bounds for our discussion here.

We can see that devoting the mind to problem-solving or trying to figure something out doesn't create suffering. Whatever problem we are trying to solve, we are doing it present time, and probably it is related to real life. Often the solution or insight that results from these efforts can make a difference in our lives.

Another example of conceptual-action is a possibility that can be quite imaginative while still aligning to what is. Creating a state might be generated conceptually but if it is consciously done in the present and for a purpose that serves the life you are living, it is an action, not an activity. Such possibilities include meditative states to calm the mind, become more present, heal yourself in some way, or whatever the goal of the meditation is. If you embark on generating states that increase awareness and sensitivity, you are also taking conceptual-actions and these actions don't create suffering but usually enhance life.

Along these lines, such imaginative states could include creating a feeling-image—for example, the body-being grounding exercise of imagining a chain connected to your center that is attached to a huge heavy lead ball hanging beneath the ground in order to develop being far more grounded in your body-mind. There are many, many other feeling-images that can serve to align your experience to a principle that generates more power and effectiveness or as a training to do so. These are not just fantasies or imagined scenarios but are using creative conceptual abilities to increase skills or life-enhancing experiences.

The list of states that can be created is long. In this regard, the field is wide-open and limited only by your inventiveness. The only requisite is that these states occur in and are about present time and serve a function that relates to life as you live it. Therefore, they are conceptual-actions that don't cause suffering. Instead, they enhance your life.

Adopting certain principles will also align mind and experience with *is*. For example, honesty demands aligning with what's true, ergo, what is. People often miss this fact—that honesty is not just about being a good person, but it is a function of what's true or actually experienced—and this pushes even our conceptual-activity to relate to life as it unfolds in real time. This clearly applies to self-honesty.

Of course, we can still "honestly" conceptualize unhealthy or dysfunctional activities, thinking they are really true. But if we are committed to pursuing what is actually true, we will discover these to be false, and then honesty demands we drop them. Even though we can make mistakes or be ignorant while being honest, it tends to push us toward what is, rather than support spinning our wheels with what isn't.

When adopting a principle, however, the principle needs to be clearly understood so that you are actually aligning with the principle and not an idea or belief that might accompany the word. There are many principles and distinctions that accomplish powerful real-life enhancement, and more of these will be addressed near the end of the book in chapters 8, "Creating New Experiential Abilities," and 9, "Powerful Life-Enhancing Principles." These are all conceptual-actions that turn *isn't* into *is*.

There are many more possibilities that push *isn't* into *is*, but what we've addressed so far gives us a solid place to start. The main question to ask is whether or not the concept you're having is related to now and the demands of real life. Is it life enhancing, known for what it is, and related to present time? Is it about now and serving life? If the answer to these questions is yes, it is conceptual-action and won't create suffering.

Notice that this excludes the myriad of conceptual-activities that aren't about life in this moment, such as comparing what you experience now with something not present but merely imagined. This domain includes fantasy, wishful thinking, desires, imagining a better life than what you have, the idea that something other than what is "should be," judging yourself, and so on. None of these enhance life or are about real life, but they do cause suffering.

Concepts that don't serve, however, can often be turned into something that does. For example, you can see that imagining a better future could be turned into creating a plan to accomplish something and a commitment to do so. This then changes it from the domain of activity to action. This makes a real difference not only in taking away comparing your life to an imagined fantasy or ideal—thus ending the suffering caused by doing that—it also tends to empower your life as you live it.

In the same vein, we can see a fantasy simply generates longing for what isn't, and in the process demeaning what is. We could transform this activity into action by changing it to a feeling-image to create results in present time. Whatever you are looking for in a fantasy, what can be created that uses the feeling-image of the fantasy to create a result in the present? If you can do this, it won't create suffering and might add something to your experience.

Considering further, there may be a relationship between a powerful and creative mind that tends to access conceptual-action and the less responsible suffering mind that seems stuck in conceptual-activities. It is interesting to consider that perhaps what makes a person a creative or powerful thinker, artist, inventor, contemplator, and so on, is using concept to great effect, spending their time and focus on conceptual-action and being in the present. Whereas those that spend too much time in conceptual-activities may also have a lack of mental control and see themselves as victim to such activities, not as responsible for them. If this latter case is so for you, then shifting activities to actions should also increase the power and effectiveness of your mind as well as increase your creativity. A win-win, decreasing suffering and increasing power and effectiveness all at the same time.

Although the often-buried core beliefs and assumptions you have may not seem like they are a function of imagination, they are really just deeper conceptual-activities. These can lead to such efforts as trying to fix yourself of ill-defined personal flaws or maladies, thinking you should reach for ideals that aren't practical with the idea that once attained they will mend you or complete you so that life will be what it "should" be. Many of them are taken for granted and just accepted as your nature or as the way life is, when they are not. They are something you are generating and they cause suffering. By becoming conscious of what they are and that you are really just spinning your wheels, you can free yourself from them and the consequences of believing in them. (We will address this domain more in chapter 7, "Beneath the Surface.")

Understanding the dramatic difference between conceptual-activity and conceptual-action gives us a power that is rare for humans. Once we grasp these two domains, we have to decide if we are going to commit to choosing one over the other. As it is, we are already committed to conceptual-activities by default. It's how our culture and probably all cultures are designed. Choosing a new path might be challenging, but with this new distinction it is now possible. At this point in the book, I want to point out that we have everything we need to end suffering. I will continue with more work, but it's important to get that we have already covered everything needed to end suffering—in case you missed that. If you did, go back and reconsider. Everything to come just supports and clarifies this foundation.

CHOOSING A PATH FORWARD

Again, only when you imagine that some experience is better than the one you are currently having does the one you are having become bad or negative. You could also imagine an experience that is far worse than what you are having and then your current experience would be seen as pleasant or good. Notice the difference between these two perspectives. Also notice there is no real reason to choose the first over the second.

We should acknowledge that we most often dwell on what could be better, not what could be worse. In this way, we create suffering rather than feel privileged to have our current real experience. What's more, when we focus on what could be worse, we usually do it as a future scenario generating worry and fear and so create suffering once again. Why do you think we choose those activities rather than others?

Why push the mind to generate stuff that creates suffering rather than satisfaction? I know, people say that it motivates them to achieve a better experience and that's why they "have" to do it. But take a look. Does it work? Do you achieve a better experience by doing that? Very likely not, and certainly not constantly or most of the time. But you do frequently, if not constantly, suffer in this way. Think about it.

What's also true is giving up this conceptual-activity doesn't at all keep you or anyone from pursuing whatever you want. As a matter of fact, you are far more likely to actually achieve something with action than you ever will with activity. It simply has to be done as outlined, with conceptual and physical actions, not conceptual-activities that go nowhere and just cause mental-emotional distress. Then you are happy with life *as is* as well as happy building something or attempting to achieve something. This is a very different world than what most of us are used to, isn't it? Notice once again that this is all created via concept.

We've touched on many examples of shifting from the dominance of conceptual-activities—or what isn't—into conceptual-actions that relate to what is. From this distinction, we learned to use concept in a way that enhances life, rather than in the ways that create unnecessary suffering as is so often the case. Most people don't understand the difference between these two domains of mental activity and the consequences for engaging one or the other. When we blur them together, much distress is created as if it's simply the cost of life, when it isn't.

It might not always be easy to stop the conceptual mischief that presses us to engage in unhealthy and detrimental mind activities. But the more we experience that they are unreal and unnecessary—that they really exist in idea-land, not real life—the more we are empowered to make this shift. Adam and Eve may have fallen into this trap and doomed the rest of us to assume that role, but we can get out of it.

OUR FEAR OF THE MUNDANE

One of the most common, often overlooked, core fears we have is being mundane. Why is that? It seems there are many moments where life feels rather mundane. More than that, from time to time most people—in those perhaps rare moments when feeling isolated and without distraction—confront a sense that they're incomplete, lacking something important, and perhaps even have a sense of personal panic from this lack that the mundane tends to draw out. Many people are quite successful at keeping this core aspect hidden from themselves because they keep their minds involved in constant distractions of some kind.

But cracks can occur in a moment of self-reflection when you're not involved with something that is keeping your mind otherwise occupied. You might see yourself and your life as meaningless at its core and in need of something, likely ill-defined, that you're lacking. This "lack" feels intolerable. It quite possibly might feel like something that must be excised from your body and mind, or fixed within you, but you find no way to do that. The fact that life offers many distractions suggests the solution to this distress is also to be found outside of yourself.

Clearly, we don't feel completely self-contained. Instead it seems as if there is something "out there" that can make our core experience better. Without some distraction, without some experience that grabs our attention and keeps us from dwelling on our unadorned state, we feel bored and incomplete. We feel stuck in this suffering and as if we have to find or attain something not inherent within our experience that will make us happy with ourselves and lives. We seem to need something from the outside to complete us.

We can see that this hope of redemption is fueled by the fact that when we fall in love, or go on a fun adventure, or are well entertained, we indeed feel good. So when such things aren't happening—and we feel dissatisfied with the sameness and lackluster experience of life without stimulation—how could we not think that we need something outside ourselves to change this distress?

This deep and overlooked but taken-for-granted form of suffering, which plagues pretty much everybody, finds itself in a description of life in the monastery from *Eat, Sleep, Sit* by Kaoru Nonomura, a Zen monk trainee:

> But now I realize that apart from a few special days now and then, life mostly consists of one dull, insignificant day after another. Human beings are attracted to drama and variety. The humdrum we hold in disdain. Wrapped up in the routines of our daily lives, we let them slide by unnoticed. But I believe that hidden in these ordinary, unremarkable routines of life is a great truth that requires our attention.
>
> By contemplating life as it is, stripped of all extraneous added value, I found I could let go of a myriad of things that have been gnawing at my mind. Through the prosaic repetition of [the Zen monastery's] exacting daily routines for washing the face, eating, defecating, and sleeping, this is the answer that I felt in my bones: accept unconditionally the fact of your life and treasure each moment of each day.

We have a very hard time grasping that there is nothing "out there" that will fix us or complete us and make us happy. There is nothing outside of us that will fix this malady. It is totally created within our own minds. We fail to question why we need something better. What's wrong with us as a being that we should need something to complete our self-experience? Resolution is not to be found in what can distract us or give us the promise of something better.

The truth is, unless you let your mind create this deep pain, it doesn't exist. It is very hard for most people to get that they are already complete. Nothing needs to be done to achieve it, except become conscious of the truth. And this truth must stand up to even the horror of being mundane.

THE SEARCH FOR MEANING

One of the more important conceptual-activities driving us is the search for meaning. We want to feel we are meaningful and have a meaningful life. This is a core desire for almost everyone. But it seems most people feel they fall short of its achievement. This is a tricky subject to tackle, especially because we are so deeply attached to its pursuit.

We want to have meaning, but often don't know how to accomplish that condition or what it would look like. From this position, we tend to reach for ideals as the answer to our problem. This does provide an imagined goal we think once attained will provide the meaning we seek. But ideals are only imagined, and they are most often unreasonable if not unattainable.

As we've seen, the creation of ideals is motivated by our deficiencies—as in our lack of meaning—and the idea that attaining ideals will fix us. They will not. The ideal is always about attaining something not had, and that makes it, by definition, something outside of our self-experience. Yet the resolution for our deficiencies can only happen within us, not without.

This lack of meaning can be tackled in many ways. You might just feel meaningless and hopeless and live life as a loser in your own mind. You could focus on some ideals that you are pursuing and this may suggest that you are on your way to attain meaning, thus giving you meaning in the interim. You might simply compare yourself to an ideal thought to be needed in order to be meaningful and find yourself wanting. You can wallow in sorrow and self-deprecation, or keep distracted with life activities setting aside the meaning of life for later, or simply assign meaning to your life or self in some way. But as we've seen, the demand and desire for meaning so often causes a deep form of suffering.

Even if we don't find meaning in the life we are living as it is, most often we are too busy with the events of life to focus on our sense of meaninglessness. In this way we keep ourselves distracted. But just like other causes of suffering, the challenge of meaning sits in the background as a constant presence, even if it's covered up most of the time. Yet in reflective moments, as with the mundane, we indeed encounter it, especially when we question our life path or how our lives are going. What's also true is the search and pursuit of meaning in life may well be the fuel that unconsciously drives many of our pursuits and decisions.

To get a clearer sense of the role meaning plays in our lives, remember our friend the rabbit. Notice the rabbit doesn't seek meaning and also doesn't suffer this malady. We might think the rabbit is just ignorant, but ignorant of what? What does he not know in this case that doesn't serve him? The need for being a meaningful rabbit? Having a meaningful rabbit life? How would that happen? We can see that the rabbit doesn't suffer at all by not being burdened with this conceptual search and need. The contrast between a rabbit and us clearly reveals all the meaningless-meaning activities our minds get caught up in.

Living each moment of life is the only meaning the rabbit needs. His life is found in what is, not what isn't. Just so, each day my cat does his same routines—calling at the window to be let in, eating, napping, calling to go outside, and so on. He doesn't seem to have any problem or concern that his life is rather mundane or that it should be any other way, and he doesn't seem to tire of the sameness or lack enthusiasm for each event of life as it occurs. Why? Perhaps a lesson for us?

The truth is life is meaningless. That is not a negative, it's just the truth. There is no inherent meaning in being a self or in being alive, or even in living a life. Meaning is applied, not found. Our cultural values and social beliefs demand meaning. If we aren't meaningful then we are considered wrong and insignificant, and this is intolerable. Yet how do we determine whether we have meaning or not?

Again, finding meaning is held as if it's accomplished from something outside ourselves. We think that meaning can be found and that it exists "out there" in some form that we need to adopt or do or achieve. Consider how this relates to what we've seen about the causes of suffering. Being entrenched in the notion that without meaning we are worthless and that meaning is achieved from outside ourselves is the source of significant suffering.

Meaning is self-created, not found. Meaning, like purpose, has to be created. We tend to think that having a purpose will give us meaning. We also think we need to find a purpose, or that purpose will come to us or be given to us, or is found in our destiny. Purpose—other than a self-agenda passing for purpose—has to be consciously created. For that to happen, we have to be responsible for creating it. But for most of us that seems a bridge too far.

As a teacher and facilitator, over the decades I have noticed that people like to be told what to do. At first, I suspect there will be a lot of pushback to this notion. People usually say they never like to be told what to do and want to be independent, in charge, and so on. But look again. Why seek out religions, spiritual practices, advice, self-help books? Why get a personal trainer or life coach, or look for the newest diet, or steps to a better life, or how to be a success, and all the other pursuits that are basically being told what to do?

I noticed early on in my career that people are rarely self-motivated. For example, after being taught a subject, students seldom took it on themselves to investigate it further and train it by themselves. For further training or investigation, they needed something like a drill sergeant to tell them what to do and when to do it. Since that wasn't a role I cherished, I threatened to set up a tape recorder in the corner barking standard instructions for them to train and put it on a loop. It is the same for training physical skill or for increasing consciousness. This lack of self-motivation and responsibility is a common phenomenon. You may be wondering why I bring it up. It is the same basic dynamic as searching for meaning.

It may seem beyond your personal abilities, but you yourself need to create whatever purpose you attribute meaning to if you want to create a meaningful life. Once created, you have to commit to living it. You can see that none of that is outside yourself. This echoes my assertion that meaning isn't found, it is created.

What do you consider meaningful? Do you see contributing to others or humanity as meaningful? Do you presume being successful at something provides meaning? Whatever you consider meaningful, then obviously you have to take action toward that end as a lifelong commitment in order to create the meaning you seek—and not just think about it. Again, this is the difference between conceptual-activity and conceptual-action.

If that doesn't do it for you, then you need to get that meaning is meaningless. Again, this doesn't mean you are meaningless as a negative, but that existence, and you, have no meaning. Grasp that you are already complete and don't need some outside influence to complete you or give you meaning. Be happy with simply being. You can give meaning to it or, like our rabbit, be completely OK with simple ordinary daily activities without looking for something else. In any case, recognize that this need for meaning creates suffering and it is all in your mind. You are complete just because you are.

> *Life has to be given a meaning because of the obvious fact*
> *that it has no meaning.*
>
> HENRY MILLER

BEING COMPLETE

You need to notice that without all the unnecessary conceptual-activity your experience is already complete in this moment. There is nothing that *should be* other than what you experience as life in present time. What's also true is there is nothing that *can* be other than what you experience as life in present time. When you totally accept and reside within your present life experience, being "incomplete" is not possible.

You might still ask, why does that have to be the case? Why is it impossible to be incomplete when your experience is all about what's true in your present life? Remember, real life is objectively occurring.

Set aside the addition of conceptual-action devoted to real life for a moment and perhaps you can more easily see this proposition by limiting real life to what is physical or biological.

An object can't be incomplete. The object is always and only what it is. So you can see that whatever is objectively occurring, it is completely and only what it is. Certainly you might say that some object should be bigger or is missing something and so is incomplete. But you also see this is something you are adding that the object does not. It is only what it is and exactly as it is. It is the same for the three-legged dog—only you say his missing leg is a problem; he is just happily living life. Therefore, in this same way, your life can't be incomplete unless you think it is.

Even the conceptual act of interpreting what is perceived as physically and biologically occurring will still be completely and only what it is. That is, if it's confined to what is presently perceived as occurring, without adding such concepts as,

> what might be better?
> where is it going?
> what does it mean?
> what's missing?
> and so on.

Those aren't perceptive interpretations of what is, they are conceptual-activities that distract from the present. When this conceptual mischief doesn't occur, the truth is seen: life is occurring as life is occurring and it is complete. Nothing else is needed and nothing else can happen. Only what happens can happen.

Because of this fact, a shift to "what is" ends the distress caused by the conceptual nonsense that creates suffering. A sense of being incomplete simply means that you are not OK as you are but in need of some imagined experience that promises to complete you.

As seen, there are many contributors to your sense of being

incomplete. When you long for something not present, you'll view your current experience as incomplete—somehow flawed, or broken, or less than, or inadequate, or what have you. Being complete means nothing is missing or needs to be fixed. This experience is not based on your circumstances but on you.

I'm not sure if this fits, but a long time ago I realized that there was no fundamental difference to the quality of life standing in the Taj Mahal or in a dirt-floored shack. Both are simply dwellings. The rest is mind. And if you don't mind, you can be happy no matter where you are.

People often think that if they accept life as is, they will give up all aspirations to attain something better. This is really just a red herring, and it is what much of our dissatisfaction is based upon. But it is just not true. There is nothing in ending suffering that requires we give up creating or building or attaining something. We simply have to make sure such "visions" are grounded in reality and based on commitment. Then our ambitions can be channeled into a reality.

Yet you need to make a distinction between drives and ambitions generated in an attempt to keep you distracted from underlying pain or simply creating something because you want to do so. Ask yourself: What motivates you to pursue attaining something? Is it the promise that it will "fix" you or make your life experience tolerable? I call pursuits based on this drive a self-agenda (something we will look into more later on). But if it isn't based on a self-agenda, you can create or attain whatever you want without it being related to avoiding suffering or trying to fix you or remedy your distress. Notice, in this way, you are also OK without attaining anything. Then you are happy with life as it is, as well as happy with whatever you may be building or creating.

When you are complete and present, the actions taken toward any pursuit don't change being complete in any way because these actions aren't taken for that reason. Unfortunately, a great deal of what is pursued by humans is done for the wrong reasons. Such drives are often based on being incomplete and trying to fix that malady.

A major motivator to our pursuits is so often a sense of being incomplete. We are motivated by such experiences as being lonely, flawed, bored, needy, empty, and so on. Being complete ends the usually unconscious undercurrents of drives and needs that create a self-agenda to resolve these distressful experiences. This frees up a huge amount of energy and attention, actions and reactions, that are no longer necessary to manage feeling incomplete. As well, it dispels the suffering caused by these efforts.

Contrary to what might seem impossible, to be complete all you need to do is get that you are already complete. Accept yourself and life exactly as they are and you are complete. Get that you don't need anything that isn't already so, the life you have is already the life you are living; there's nothing missing and nothing needed that isn't there—unless you add conceptual-activities. So don't.

> *I am happy because I want nothing from anyone. I do not care about money. Decorations, titles or distinctions mean nothing to me. I do not crave praise. I claim credit for nothing. A happy man is too satisfied with the present to dwell too much on the future.*
>
> ALBERT EINSTEIN

Overriding the impulse to add conceptual-activities might seem difficult. So perhaps understanding the real nature of perspective could help provide some space to challenge your own mind. At the risk of pushing the envelope too far and losing your attention, I want to go down another existential road, the ignorance of which has a great deal to do with remaining stuck in experiences of suffering.

NO PERSPECTIVE IS TRUE

All humans view the world a certain way. Each of us has a perspective about life and how it all goes down. We view life—what's right and wrong, good and bad—based on self-concerns and self-interests formulated around the belief systems and values we've adopted.

No matter what you think is going on here, in the world and in your life, it will be based on your perspective—how you view it and why you view it that way. It will be formed around a framework built from your history, beliefs, assumptions, values, culture, and so on. Most people have a hard time clearly discerning their own perspective because to them it seems they are just observing the world. But this is far from true. Looking more carefully you should see that you have a particular viewpoint and specific perspectives of the way it all is. The thing is no perspective, no view, is true.

I know this is likely not going to be a popular assertion. Yet it's not possible that any view can be true. This might be impossibly tricky to get, because we only get stuff through the filter of our perspectives. But we can see that any perspective is based on the stuff mentioned above and that stuff is all invented and adopted by humanity, our culture, our family, and mostly ourselves. This limits the view to made-up stuff, not to what's inherently true. And all perspectives are conceptual in nature. It is "knowledge" formed in the mind and interpreted by an already biased individual. In this way, no perspective can actually be true.

Of course, we could be more or less devoted to pursuing what's true. We might work hard to be honest and to perceive what's true as best we can. And this will be a much more powerful and different experience than any other. But even then, our view can never match the existential nature of reality. If for no other reason, a view is always one-sided.

For example, we view an object from only one perspective, one side, and can only see what's visible to us from that perspective, that physical point of view. We don't see the other side of it or under it, and so on. If we could view the object from every angle and every side infinitely, we would have more information and a much different perspective about it. But even then, we still don't see it from the inside, nor do we see its real nature, or see it for-itself. It is the same for our perspectives on reality. Intellectually we can understand this limitation, even though we can't transcend it. But our challenge is even trickier than that.

Our subjective perceptions might be up for grabs as to their ultimate validity, but we have to admit that the objective world must be without alteration and so be what's true, don't we? Well, maybe not. Certainly, there is a seemingly solid foundation offered by the physical world and we respect its nature as not subject to the whims of mind and perspective.

Yet we see that we add a great deal to what we perceive no matter how much or how little information or data we have about it. Just as we are unable to see objective reality from every view-point, inside and out, we have to admit that an ant or a bird or any other creature will not see the same thing as we do. This tells us our perceived reality is always self-created and not simply a reflection of what is, but a function of the viewer.

Beyond these limitations, it's not possible for anything formed and limited to represent the real nature of existence. No perspective can occur without it being formed and so limited. But for you to personally experience this may seem out of reach or perhaps seem to be just nonsense. I appreciate that sentiment. Yet you still may be able to recognize that whatever perspective you have in itself is not absolute or completely free from bias. You can also grasp that your particular perspective could change, and probably has changed from time to time, and so can't be inherently or existentially true.

If you can experience this to some degree you can see how it relates to your suffering. Each conceptual-activity that generates suffering is always wed to a perspective. Sometimes a perspective seems to demand certain reactions, and you may have difficulty giving up particular concepts imagined to be true or necessary. So grasping that none of it is ultimately true can go a long way toward giving you the space to change your mind and let it go.

⇘

If there is no self, there is no suffering.
If there is no mind, there is no suffering.
If there is no self-mind, there is no suffering.

Absent these activities, suffering doesn't exist. Think about it. That should give us pause about idealizing both self and mind. We think that self and mind are existential realities and are necessary core aspects of life. But entertaining the assertion that neither of these are necessary or real—and even as they occur, they don't need to remain inviolate—is a big leap to make. This is why we went through the assertions earlier that both the inner-self and mind are inventions. Such understanding creates the possibility of challenging these fundamental aspects of our experience.

Knowing that our individual perspective is just a view and not existentially true helps modify the assumption that the activities of self and mind are always correct and necessary. They are just doing a job, and often the way they go about that job is not necessary or most effective.

It might seem like our perspectives are not really all that important to our experience or actions. But I suggest that isn't so. How we hold things determines our entire relationship to life.

As a very minor example, I remember seeing a commercial once that was trying to be inspirational. From my perspective, I thought they got it completely wrong. Clearly, they were catering to people's emotional sense of fantasy. Their assertion was: Why is the American dream called a dream and not a plan or a goal? Then they pushed the idea that in a dream you can imagine all sorts of things in an unlimited way. True, but they are missing the point.

In my view, a plan and goal would be a much better option. Why? Because plan and goal are conceptual-action, but dream evokes only conceptual-activity. Regardless of what is imagined, committing to a plan or goal is far more powerful and realistic. The dream is a fantasy and is not about taking action that makes a difference and only creates disappointment and dissatisfaction because it is focusing on what isn't, without it being grounded in committed action. My vote would be for the American plan and goal, not the dream.

We can see how such differing views will strongly influence our relationship to life. But again, although some perspectives are more empowering or effective in real life, none are actually true. Once we know this, when we are stuck with some emotion or mood or outlook that causes distress and we don't seem to be able to get our feet under us to manage this experience well, it is useful to know that even our strongest and most demanding view is not in itself true. In this way, we are better equipped to drop it, regardless of overwhelming pressures to stay with it.

It is very useful to get that your mind is not always your best friend. Although it may be difficult to grasp and admit, it is powerful to acknowledge that in so many ways you're "fucked in the head." This simply means that your mind has been programmed to automatically generate an endless stream of suffering-causing activities. It is also very useful to create some humor around your suffering. Admitting you're fucked in the head should be a comedic act. If not, it's likely to just create more drama and cause suffering. Once you admit that your mind often goes down unfruitful roads and can laugh at your own folly, it gives you a lot more space to let go of this ridiculous behavior.

Life is 10% what happens to you and 90% how you react to it.

CHARLES R. SWINDOLL

SUFFERING AND CONSCIOUSNESS

Transcending the Meaning of Feelings

We've seen there are many feeling-states that we suffer, and we often have difficulty seeing the real purpose behind having such feelings. It is useful to understand why these feelings exist. Toward that end, we need to get to the bottom and acknowledge—independent of our self-needs—what any feeling or impulse is really up to, even if it is uncomfortable for us to do so. Then we can deal with them more successfully.

Since sometimes we get caught up in our emotions, it can be difficult to question them to discover their purpose. Although all emotions have the same root purpose, which is self-survival, each has a specific purpose to orient us and motivate us to take particular actions. This is simply saying that the purpose of everything arising within us serves to manage life.

❧

There is no suffering without self-survival.

Think of it this way, your body has many physiological activities to keep you alive, most of which go on without your knowledge. You also breathe regularly, eat, sleep, and so on, as your body dictates. You can see that these activities exist to keep you alive, even though they mostly arise either without your knowledge or, for volitional actions, without your resistance. These activities are necessary for life. But what is added by the mind is not and can also be detrimental. For example, you may need to eat, but if you are neurotic or have buried emotional pain, you might overeat and become obese. This is not only unnecessary for life, it is unhealthy for life.

It is the same basic drive for the mental-emotional mischief that strongly pushes us in various directions. We experience some thoughts as if they are as necessary and compelling as breathing. But in reality, they are simply activities we're generating conceptually and are often not necessary or healthy. It is difficult for most of us to see these drives and impulses for what they are.

Yet shy of grasping why a feeling occurs, it is possible to simply feel it as a feeling without adding anything to it. When some feeling or sensation comes our way, the mind will interpret what it is, what it means to us, and how we should relate to it. From this process, a reaction to the feeling arises. This happens extremely fast and seamlessly, but it does happen.

For example, if you are feeling distress about some feeling-sensation it is because your brain reads this feeling-sensation as uncomfortable and requires you to adopt a disposition of distress and then try to conjure up a solution to get out of the distress. If no viable solution is forthcoming, you remain in a condition of suffering.

Yet it is also possible to simply perceive the feeling and leave it alone. In other words, deliberately override the automatic activities that generate this distress. Then the feeling is just a feeling and there is no distress. This can be done with any emotion or other feelings that are uncomfortable.

Still, the mind is relentless and will continue to do its job because it has been trained that way over a lifetime. So once freed of some distress, you're likely to slip back into it because the mind will continue to work. Remember, its job is to help you survive, and it does that by discerning good and bad experiences and producing feelings and reactions to motivate you to find ways to embrace the good and avoid or manage the bad. That's its job.

But the mind is filled with mistaken or dysfunctional beliefs and assumptions and inaccurate knowledge, and these form the basis for its decisions. So unnecessary pain and suffering is automatically generated because of the "information" fed into it—as we saw in chapter 4, "Mental Activities behind Most Forms of Suffering."

When we subtract the meaning from any feeling, it becomes just a feeling and doesn't have any power to motivate us or put us in distress. Unfortunately, for most of us this has to be done willfully and as soon as the will to do it subsides, the automatic tendencies take over. But perhaps if we do it often enough and long enough, it too can become a more automatic disposition and ability.

To be clear, grasping the nature and purpose of our feeling-states doesn't necessarily create a bliss of freedom—that is rare and doesn't seem likely to happen frequently for humans. It simply allows an "understanding" that can modify the overwhelming nature of such experiences. Choosing to temporarily transcend these forces is always available. Yet, when in the middle of a strong and demanding feeling-state, that option is rarely taken because self-survival tends to overwhelm us. Still, the real possibility that you could grasp and step outside of what is taking place—even while you feel victim to it—can make a difference in your relationship to the forces that are pushing you around.

Clearly, most people seem to suffer mental-emotional angst from time to time. Sometimes this is significant and feels like reality and life are disturbingly depressing in some way. Living solely within the mind gives no relief from this activity because the activity is generated entirely by the mind. When you can focus on, or better yet be conscious of, being the source of mind and experience and not those activities themselves, you free yourself from this whole activity altogether.

You can make this shift by meditating on you as the source—being the root of your experience and not the experience itself—or by creating the possibility of directly experiencing your true nature through contemplation. Either way, your mental activity calms down as your focus moves from generating mental distress to abiding in being the source of that activity. Without creating this possibility, you are stuck in whatever dismaying outlook and perspective has arisen. Yet even if you are stuck, you can still shift to feeling whatever you're feeling as just a feeling.

Whatever distressful perspective you experience, no matter what it is, is not true; it is a fabrication you are making up. If it causes suffering, it's useful to get this. In the end, it is unnecessary and unreal and so you can simply let it go—you can stop this sound and fury, or at least detach from it. You may feel unable to do this, as if the arising negative perspective is just the case and you have no choice but to endure it.

Imagine someone is telling you a very sad tale of woe and misery and you feel like crying at their undeserved distress. Then imagine they suddenly tell you they were lying, that they just made up the story. What would happen? You can see the emotion would suddenly dissolve as a reality and you are instantly freed from it. This shows you how to let go of your own stuff. Get that it is a fabrication, a story you're telling yourself—no matter how sophisticated or background it is—and it is unnecessary. Then you can just give it up wholesale.

The Role of Truth

How do you become conscious of such things as these? This domain of "knowledge" might seem inaccessible to most people. Such consciousness starts by working to understand and directly experience what's true with a subject, like discovering the nature of emotions, or what causes suffering, and the like. But such a pursuit must start from the ground up. In other words, you must seek the truth, not look for a result.

Although you likely would pursue becoming conscious to help you in some way, your investigation and contemplation shouldn't relate to such goals. If you pursue the truth to improve or gain value, you are pursuing the wrong thing and so won't grasp what's actually true. Suffering is a personal problem. Don't burden discovering the truth with solving that problem. Becoming more conscious of the realities behind suffering or just your experience in general increases your ability to change or manage them. Simply don't confuse discovering truth as being self-serving.

It may be difficult to suspend your self-concerns and drives in order to investigate the matter independent of what it might do for you, but it is necessary if you're going to really grasp the dynamics in which you are stuck and get free of them. First things first. Even if the only reason you pursue increasing your consciousness is to help you in some way, don't focus on what you imagine you'll get out of it because that will get in the way of any real discovery. Get what's true first, then see if it makes a difference in what you can do.

As we've seen, the kind of shift it takes to end suffering depends on changing our minds. It might be the case that most of us don't have any desire to change our minds or perhaps don't seem to have the ability to do so. The desire is a choice and is probably stuck in the idea that all that mind activity is necessary. So this idea would have to be challenged.

As for the capacity, the next section could improve your understanding of your mental "gears" and how they work, helping you increase your ability to control your mind. This continuing investigation might seem too abstracted from your immediate concerns. Yet as an analogy, consider that learning how a washing machine works doesn't get your clothes clean, and if clean clothes are your focus the learning seems useless. But if the machine is tearing up your clothes, then learning how to repair it or change how it operates is in order. Creating such abilities can't happen without investigation and learning.

Since so much of our suffering and distress is produced by processes and dynamics that are often unclear or obscure, it is useful to delve more deeply into how these activities and experiences occur, as well as offer some alternative ways of viewing them. Most people are not very sensitive to what they themselves are doing and the nature or dynamics of the processes that they undertake and generate. A lot of this goes on automatically and in the background and so goes unnoticed but still forms the foundation of how our experience is created. Becoming more conscious of these dynamics can also help you learn to control your mind and understand how and in what ways you are responsible for your experience.

We are healed from suffering only by experiencing it to the full.

MARCEL PROUST

PART III

❧

Investigating Our Experience

I often speak about existential matters—as found in other books and some of what I've said in the first chapters here—and these are important matters that require deep understanding or direct consciousness in order to grasp. Yet I also want to offer more observations about the common experiences in which we live and how they work.

Certainly, regarding what is already established in our experience, an existential view of these activities allows us to create insights that can transform that same experience. When we bore down into overlooked elements of our experience, what we discover can make a real difference in our lives. As we saw with all the concepts that create suffering, what we do with our minds makes a big difference in how our experience turns out. Having a deeper experiential understanding of how the mind works gives us a greater ability to control it and to change those conceptual-activities where it's useful to do so. In this section, we will address such work.

❧

You think and live as if you are a particular "person,"
but it doesn't have to remain that way.

CHAPTER SIX

About Mind

THINKING

What you think, and how you think it, makes a significant difference in your overall experience. But we take our thinking for granted and overlook the possibility that our thinking may not be valid or useful. Of course, we might entertain the idea that something we think could be wrong, but such thoughts are rare. Mostly we don't look in that direction. We assume that what we do mentally is necessary and accurate just because that's what we're doing.

Of course, now we can see that our thinking can generate suffering. Normally, most people just don't know why this happens. Since most often we attribute circumstance as the cause of our discomfort we don't tend to consider our own thinking could actually be the cause. The kind of thinking that causes suffering is a lot like faith-based thinking. We might consider the results of faith-based thinking to be based on reality and necessary, harmless, or just how life goes. But this is like basing conceptual-activity on blind faith—not a good idea. In order to break free of this, we are better served by challenging such thinking.

One of the first actions to take toward that end is to question the validity of your own thinking. Since your thoughts are usually taken for granted as valid in and of themselves, it may seem odd to consider that they may not be. But you have many, many thoughts that aren't based on fact or reason or objective reality, but on imagination and desire and so forth. These thoughts shouldn't be considered valid. If your thoughts seem inherently valid, what method could you use to discover any invalidity?

Beliefs and assumptions, which are insular and self-referencing by nature, tend to dominate what one thinks. By making a distinction between what is objectively true and what is simply a belief or assumption, you have a way to proceed toward clarity. You'll need to be vigilant about noticing when your thoughts are just subjective musings, internal manipulations, biased in some way, or are influenced by preference or fear. To create a foundation for clarity, make thoughts that are influenced by any of these kinds of activities distinct from what is true prior to or free from those activities. In this way, you can question your thinking and move in the direction of becoming clearer as to the validity of your thoughts.

In order for a thought to be "valid" it should be based on fact, honest experience, or powerful reflective observations free of bias or spin. Ask yourself questions such as,

> Are these thoughts founded on what is objectively true, factually based, or in your best assessment, are they based on reason and objectivity?
> Are they founded on honesty?
> Are they universally empowering?
> Are they free from bias or distortion?

If the answer to these questions is affirmative, you could call those thoughts credible, legitimate, or useful. Being clear as to which thoughts are sound, grounded, or effective, and which are not—thoughts that are just a guess, fantasy, belief, or manipulation—you can begin to develop clarity in your thinking.

Instead of being buffeted around within a world of reactive mind, with clear discernment you can better deal with each circumstance or idea openly and without presumption. At first this is easier said than done. But over time it can become natural, and once it becomes more automatic, the main remaining impediment is your own agenda of desires and fears. Can you see the work that has to be done? If so, ask yourself if you're going to do it or just read about it.

In trying to sort out which forms of thinking are empowering and valid we should fully acknowledge that our own reactions to, and judgments of, anything encountered distorts our thinking and interpretation. When we react and judge we end up making knee-jerk decisions based on beliefs, history, and our own perspective, thus decreasing our effectiveness.

Remember, what we believe is often strongly and mistakenly thought to be true. Work needs to be done to challenge even our most cherished or long-held beliefs. This automatic propensity to bias our interpretations in this way definitely influences our thinking. In the end this causes dysfunctional and disempowering experiences.

We have seen over and over again that the content of our minds generates distress as well as good feelings. Trying to use the mind to resolve all life's conundrums by trying to find "the answers" results in intellectual conclusions that usually end up being circular and go nowhere. Perhaps, at best, you can craft a philosophy that serves you by providing a place upon which to stand to approach life. That is, if you craft a good one. If you do, it might be useful for helping you to feel good, but then adopting a religion could do the same thing.

Of course, given that religions may not be well suited for your life, you might try to make one for yourself. But your philosophy is only a fabrication, like a religion, and if you don't truly believe in it and throw yourself into it completely it won't work. On the other hand, there is another route. You don't have to make something up, you can discover what's true for yourself. You can also experience life-enhancing principles that work much better to channel your life activities because they aren't just mental noise generated by the self-mind. They are principles applicable to the very reality in which we all live—more on that possibility in part 4.

This is different from fabricating intellectual conclusions or beliefs, and since a principle is true and grounded in reality you don't have to believe in it and it can't be wrong. Sounds fishy or too good to be true, doesn't it? That's because all we've ever been taught or encountered in this domain is secondhand or intellectual musings. But there is another possibility: it is learning to think differently by investigating and directly experiencing what's true or possible in a grounded way.

Consider that the way you think isn't all that's possible. In trying to press your thinking toward new levels and abilities, it might be useful to visit a kind of thinking that is virtually unknown to most people. Most of the time thinking is dominated by intellect, psychology, and emotion. This pushes you down ruts that make your thinking limited and predictable.

EXISTENTIAL THINKING

You have heard me using the word "existential" more than once already in this book. I suspect I may have a rather unique perspective on this distinction (know that it is not related to existentialism). So let me see if I can clarify what that is.

When I say existential, I mean "of existence," what something is just because it is, prior to adding any interpretation, use, or value it might have for us. When we set out to grasp the existential nature of something, we are trying to grasp what it is in its most basic form. This form of investigation or "thinking" begins without assumption and so is not founded on any preconceptions. Instead, it starts from a base of nothing or not-knowing, a blank slate, so to speak. It might be difficult to know when you are truly free of all assumptions, but to do your best to enact this principle you need to keep an eye out for any overlooked assumptions or beliefs influencing your thinking, experience, or investigation.

From this openness, you can now consider the origins or nature of the mere existence of something. What is it, why is it, what is its purpose for existing, what is its nature? These are all questions tackled with such investigative thinking. Contemplation, investigation, and an open probing into the matter are foundational to this kind of thinking. It isn't a fuzzy or careless musing, it's a form of solving overlooked ignorance and seeking insight. The outcome of such thinking is always, in some way, an increase in consciousness.

This might sound like a powerful form of "thinking" but most people don't know it's even possible. So how is it done? Answering that question is the same act as creating such thinking.

First, you'd probably have to start with the notion that it isn't like the thinking you normally do. There's a lot of silence and "staring" into the matter. Sounds a bit like contemplation, doesn't it? A contemplative attitude is certainly a contributing aspect, but I still see it as a form of thinking rather than simply contemplating. That's because this effort requires mental activity, and this activity is directed toward understanding the nature and purpose of the existence of any aspect of the world in which we live.

We begin this effort by focusing on a subject. What is fear or desire, for example, or even what is emotion itself? Perhaps we look into what is embarrassment, why does it exist, what is it doing? Maybe we consider what is thought, or society, or culture? We could hone in on everything that comprises an act of perception, or the mind of a tree, the nature of language, the principles behind science or reason. Pretty much anything that in the end is a human invention, something generated by humans or simply experienced by us. This is why I consider it a form of thinking or mental activity that in some sense is close to but not solely contemplation. This can be a tricky distinction that finds blurry edges, so let's see if I can clarify further.

Contemplation isn't about mental activity, although mental activity may well take place while contemplating. This is because here we are usually focusing on becoming conscious of the absolute nature of something that seemingly exists as an inherent aspect of reality outside of anything invented and even beyond our perceptive-experience of it. What is an object, what am I, what is life, what is existence itself, are all questions in this domain. Yet it is within our experience that we determine what is an inherent aspect of existence and what is an invented one. Here we run into our blurring.

We might consider our "selves" inherently existing, only to find, through contemplation, that we are an invention. Or we might consider some self-assumption as existential and inherent and discover it is not, that it is just a thought. One indicator that something may not be existential but an invention is whether it didn't exist as part of the human experience at some point in time and then it did, or if it comes or goes at various times, or if it exists only to serve a purpose and not just because it "is."

As examples, we can see that language didn't exist for us at some point and so was created, that emotions or thoughts come and go, and religion exists only to serve a purpose. With both contemplation and existential thinking, we should be able to discover the truth about any and all aspects that we experience as our world, and perhaps even discover or become conscious of something that has never been experienced by anyone heretofore.

EMOTION

In our personal world, emotions indicate to us how life is going and motivate us to take actions related to these feelings. As we saw in the section on suffering, emotional dispositions dominate our experience in this domain. We generally hold these emotions and suffering as if they are circumstantially derived, only to find out they exist because of mental activities we are doing.

If we perceive our emotions as caused by circumstance, however, they appear as simply reactions created by the environment. Even though most people relate to emotions in this way, there is also a modicum of personal responsibility sprinkled in. This is seen in the attitude that one might be "over the top" with some emotional reaction, such as "I shouldn't be so angry," or "I have to get past my fears," and so on. These two perspectives reveal that we may have conflicting views on our relationship to emotions.

Although generally we live as if circumstances cause our reactions, at the same time many of us hold that we have some responsibility or control in how much we react. The perspective that emotions are caused by circumstance is our foundation, but on top of this we often struggle to alter our relationship to them. This shows up in trying to control our behavior and in our ability to suppress or adjust the strength of our feelings.

In the first perspective, we blame the reactions on others or circumstance. In the latter view, we may blame ourselves—at least for not controlling our emotions better—and then either try to suppress or modify our reaction or our behavior or attempt to compensate for or excuse our choices in some way. If instead we could experience how we are creating emotions, then not doing them or changing them becomes possible and accessible, and also our responsibility.

Again, the central thing to get about emotions is that they're always relating to the self—as are all perceptive-experiences. This is done by automatically relating whatever is encountered—objectively or subjectively—to what it means to you personally, determining whether it's good or bad, and from this information you generate an emotion to move you in a direction your mind assesses is consistent with your needs in some way.

Most of this is done subconsciously, automatically, and at lightning speeds, but it is useful to at least intellectually remember how it works. Emotions, feeling-impulses, and drives of various kinds are what steer your navigation through life. When negative emotions arise, it's because your well-being is assessed as threatened in some way, and when positive emotions arise your well-being is assessed as unfolding successfully.

Of course, it's quite a complex system, but if you pulled all self-concerns out of the picture you would find that whatever current emotion you're having is unnecessary. This knowledge alone can make a difference in your level of emotional freedom and control. Yet the self is central to all of your experiences, and its influence is so strong that the tendency is not to question your emotions but to succumb to them. It is not uncommon to get swept away by emotions in a way that is unnecessarily negative. So if you can grasp that you generate emotions—how and why—you can perhaps better modify them, or at least your behavior in expressing them.

If you look at the work done regarding specific forms of suffering, you can see that when you eliminate the concepts that generate such emotional distress, those painful experiences disappear. This is true of all emotions. When it comes to positive feelings you'll likely have no incentive to investigate them and certainly not to eliminate them. Nevertheless, it is possible to find the root and components to all emotions.

Of course, you may have some feeling that you aren't clear about— is it anger, hurt, fear? If your emotion is unclear it might be difficult to discern what the mind is doing to produce such feelings. But it is there. Clarify what you are feeling and then look into what concepts are occurring that produce those reactions. Every emotion has a root cause that begins in the mind, and human emotions have mental components necessary to produce them. You can discover what these are if you use existential investigation and contemplation. I delve into this in more detail with a cross section of major emotional dynamics in *The Book of Not Knowing* and in *Pursuing Consciousness*, so I won't go down that road here.

Yet again—because it is likely to be overlooked or missed, I repeat— if you take your self out of the equation, and stop relating what you perceive to your self, the emotion lifts. To say it another way that may be easier to hear for some people, if you stop taking it personally you won't get upset. Imagine a scene where someone says something to you that you find offensive or embarrassing or intimidating. Notice it is only offensive, embarrassing, or intimidating to you. If you weren't a consideration, if you didn't automatically hear these comments as related to you or what they mean to you—even if they're directed at you—you would have no such reactions, would you? They would simply be comments made that had nothing to do with you because you didn't make yourself the issue.

Although it is possible to eliminate an emotion, or even a kind or a domain of emotions, this isn't to say that you'll not be involved in an emotional world at all. You'll continue to relate stuff to yourself— that tends to be automatic, even though it can be overridden—and likely indulge many emotional dispositions because the emotional aspect of being human is central to social interactions. But getting caught up in them mindlessly without knowing how they get created is disempowering.

Through consciously grasping that you are generating your emotions in this way, the possibility arises you could eliminate emotional reactivity. But it does take controlling your mind. The main goal here is to move your mind into alignment with the fact that you are generating your emotions. Let's do some work on that.

RETHINKING EMOTION

It appears that the biggest difference in managing our emotions comes about when we experience that they're of our own making. We overlook the fact that if our minds want to generate negative emotions then it is something we *want* to do for some reason. So why resist it?

This is probably a new idea because emotions are founded on negative and positive feedback in order to push us in self-serving directions as we navigate through life. But if we get that even the negative feelings are generated to serve us and that we are choosing to create these feelings, we could accept and embrace these negative feelings because we understand they are something we want to do.

One way to look at negative emotions can be found in something I have created in the martial world. When two magnets are close with a positive and negative charge, they will be attracted and pulled together, but when the charges are the same they will be repulsed. Using this basic idea, one can create a field of feeling-awareness around oneself that senses potential danger or action from another that is as palpable as feeling wind blowing on the body. This feeling can move a body out of harm's way much faster and with more precision than intellect can manage. It is feeling the negative or repulsive aspect that is of value in this case.

As an analogy, I liken this ability to the old Buddhist Shaolin temple, where a graduating monk had to go through a path containing statues and whatnot that were triggered to attack as he passed. If he could navigate through this gauntlet successfully he could leave, if not, he ended up in the infirmary. Imagine if all the various weapons and fists that were thrown at him were made of iron with a positive charge. If he could put on a magnetic suit also with a positive charge that repulsed this iron, he could almost sleepwalk through the gauntlet successfully because the magnetic forces would push him away from any incoming danger. In this way, we see the negative charge as serving us and so embrace it completely.

I know it is different with emotions, but this gives us a place to start. Because negative emotions are generated to motivate us to take action to avoid, handle, or eliminate this feeling, we see it as unwanted but forget that it is also something we want. If we're generating them, then we must want to do so on some level. As unlikely as that is for us to grasp in a deep enough way to allow us to really control our emotions, it still offers an overlooked possibility that might help shift our experience of and reaction to emotions.

Beyond wanting or not, how we view an emotion changes dramatically our experience of it. For example, being afraid of fear amplifies the fear and even produces it when it's not warranted. If we can shift our disposition toward a negative emotion to one of not resisting it and even go further and grasp it as something we want for whatever reason, or allow it to be just a feeling without meaning or motivation, the badness of it disappears.

If we can shift to the disposition that we are generating our emotions and instead of acting them out or resisting them we accept them and accept responsibility for them, we won't be as affected by them as we might otherwise be. This shift requires that we put ourselves in the driver's seat. We really have to experience not only that we're generating them but be conscious of doing so in the very moments we're doing it.

"Catching ourselves in the act" from time to time or in retrospect may validate the assertion that we indeed create our own emotions, but in order to master this domain we'd need to move into the very place of generating them *as* we do so. That requires a very different relationship to how we hold being an emotional person. Can you imagine such a difference?

As I mentioned, normally your emotions are generated from relating incoming perceptive data—both objective and subjective—to your overall well-being or survival. This is a mechanical process the workings of which don't require any depth of consciousness. Imagine being conscious of the whole process as it unfolds and instead of letting it crank away automatically, you eliminate what may be dysfunctional or unhealthy—such as conceptual-activities that create unnecessary suffering—and consciously steer both interpretation and emotional processes to serve a newly created purpose. Try to imagine what might change in your experience if you could do that.

It may also be possible to simply create feeling-states from nothing, either to serve a social interaction or to generate an internal state to accomplish some end. At some point, you may be able to transcend emotional reactions altogether and just abide in an open feeling-sense that is more about freedom than about feeling. Of course, this is way easier said than done (if it's not done). It's unlikely to occur for anyone without very serious attention and commitment and lots of work and training, and you'd have to invent some reason to do so.

Understanding the workings behind our emotions gives us the opportunity to make this change. But it doesn't itself make the change or make it easy. We must confront a mind that is entrenched in its ways and determined to proceed as it has. This is what it has been trained to do. To change that takes more training, equal to the amount put into the automatic reactions and views that built it in the first place.

Toward the end of retraining the mind, there are practical and doable paths to begin generating a new relationship to emotions. Perhaps a first goal toward mastering emotions would be to enter a practice of investigating and playing with them in various ways, as in the following exercise. Of course, doing such an exercise will interrupt managing life as usual, but that is what the exercise is about.

Mastering Emotions Exercise

First, feel whatever emotion grabs your attention but without attributing meaning or being motivated by it. This may take some doing because meaning comes with emotion and its purpose is to motivate. Yet you can turn the emotion into a present feeling-state by focusing on the feeling rather than the implications for it being there.

Once you can do that, you'll relate to the feeling differently. Although the emotion may still be there, it won't have the influence it once did, and you'll be closer to noticing that it's something you're doing, or at least something you are just feeling.

The next step is to question: Why does it exist? Why in the world would such a feeling-state arise? You'll have to stop just accepting it as a given, drop cultural assumptions about it, and question it from the ground up. What is the purpose for having this particular feeling? What is it doing? Why is it there?

You can intellectually probe into it and figure out what it's motivating you to do. From there you should be able to experience the reality of this motivation, grasping that it is arising to serve a purpose—much like feeling motivated to burp or to lift a cup to take a drink.

If you probe even deeper, you can also ask: Why do you need that activity at all? What do you unconsciously believe or assume that has you thinking this activity is needed to manage life? Perhaps there is an existential assumption—some self-aspect held to be an inherent element of your nature—lying beneath the surface that is overlooked or even deliberately ignored.

Once you find whatever purpose drives the emotion to arise, you have a better shot at mastering it. But whether you discover the purpose for it or not, one practice I highly recommend is to change the emotion on the spot.

As a practice, when you find yourself stuck in any emotion, practice switching to a different dissimilar emotion, and then another, and again another, and perhaps another. Maybe you feel angry, so switch to feeling loving, then sadness, fear, and joy. Each time you have some emotion, practice having several different and unlikely emotions right then and there.

At first you may think you can't do that or that you have to find or imagine some circumstance to evoke a new emotional reaction. This isn't necessary. Perhaps you can use imagination to get you started, but eventually you should find that you can create a new emotion just by creating it, and you can make it feel genuine.

As you get good at this practice, cycling through several emotions whenever any significant one arises, you'll not only develop a greater ease at doing it, you'll obviously begin to grasp in your brain that you are creating them all—since clearly you are. In this way, you begin to master emotions rather than just being at the effect of them.

Beyond working with the manifestation and experience of emotions, it is also useful to consider the source that produces patterns of personal characteristics and reactivity. This doesn't refer to simply having an emotion from time to time; it's about patterns that you personally repeat and are driven to repeat. This source I call existential assumptions—as mentioned previously—and bottom lines. These core beliefs lead to the development of a self-agenda dedicated to trying to resolve the existential self-assumptions that are held as personal maladies.

I have communicated about this domain of experience—which is usually hidden from view—in other books (see *The Book of Not Knowing*, chapter 22), so I won't go into detail here. But some clarification about this domain and its role in creating the characteristic mental-emotional states that influence your life to a significant degree might be in order.

> *I assumed I'd become a happy old man when I aged. But it has become clear that if I keep being an angry young man, I will be an angry old man. So, I better start practicing happiness now!*
>
> DOUG CHAMBERS

CHAPTER SEVEN

Beneath the Surface

CLARIFYING EXISTENTIAL ASSUMPTIONS AND BOTTOM LINES

There are ideations or assumptions that go on beneath the surface of our awareness. As we saw earlier, there are root ideations sourcing conceptual-activities that lead to various forms of suffering. Some of these can exist in a conceptual domain that isn't easily viewable. I have called this domain "existential assumptions," so perhaps I should clarify a bit what those are.

We readily see various people having different characteristic ways of approaching life. Some seem unhealthy or less effective than others. These characteristic patterns occur as a rather constant way of being. Examples might include being shy, mean, aggressive, timid, demanding, flaky, devious, arrogant, controlling, driven, obsessive, paranoid, cloying, sour, indecisive, aloof, grumpy, dismissive, superficial, nice, rude, and on and on. Just bring to mind many people you know and you can easily find examples. Notice they are quite common. Here we're considering why they exist.

Since I have explained this domain in detail in other books, I will only briefly outline it here. Existential assumptions are core beliefs that infuse a person's sense of being and are held as an aspect of one's existence. These assumptions influence one's entire self-experience and life, yet usually go overlooked and aren't seen for what they are. Many of them cause various forms of suffering and keep us stuck in a fruitless pursuit of resolution that will never happen in the way we pursue it. This pursuit is called a self-agenda.

The mind commonly doesn't look in this direction because such an assumption about oneself is taken for granted. Instead, attention in regard to such self-aspects is focused on managing them, not inspecting them. The drives and impulses that arise to manage this existential assumption are known, but the motivation for them, the assumption itself, is usually not. You might notice you have a pattern of being some way but don't know why, and so it's simply chalked up to "it's just the way I am."

The root relationship to an existential assumption is called a bottom line. This also goes unnoticed in favor of the basic strategy undertaken to manage life in relation to this root—this strategy is what I call a self-agenda. For example, if you have a buried assumption that your being has no inherent value, the root relationship, or bottom line, may be that you are not good enough, not worthwhile. Your strategy to manage this "defect" in your person might be to endlessly try to prove you are valuable by being nice, being successful, being helpful, and so on. But your strategy could just as easily be being superior, finding ways to be in control of interactions or projects, or having a dominant personality. Your unconscious strategy could also be to endlessly pursue distractions to keep you from confronting this aspect and plunging you into depression, or you could become a bum, or wallow in self-pity.

The point is, there are many possible strategies one could adopt that can be completely different or even opposite in nature but are still based on this same root and assumption. It just depends on how your self-mind decides to try to resolve what's held as a malady of your very person. As we've seen, many of these "solutions" end up causing more suffering than the assumption itself.

Clearly, human "strategies" to manage such assumptions can show up in all sorts of ways. For example, depending on what you unconsciously assume is true of your being at its core, you could be generally shy, aggressive, fearful, outgoing, demanding, controlling, self-pitying, angry, volatile, withholding, erratic, deceitful, moody, selfish, arrogant, sloppy, irresponsible, or what have you. Although people think such characteristics are simply a part of their selves, these are actually all "strategies" to manage life—adopted by the self, most often unconsciously—to which you cling as a necessary aspect of how you relate to life.

An analogy that might serve to show how this works and get free of it can be found in a demonstration I have often used in workshops. Grabbing a doorknob—representing holding on to an unrecognized assumption—I show that I am quite limited when it comes to movement. My ambition is to be a dancer but even though I see other people dancing and twirling and moving about, try as I might I fail to be able to do those things. I don't know why. I assume it's just a character flaw in my person or some inherent defect in me.

The only way I can free myself of this condition is to *grab* the doorknob. That is to say, since I don't experience what I am doing, I need to experience what I am doing—in this case, that's grabbing the doorknob. Once I become conscious that I am actually grabbing the doorknob, only then can I stop that action and let go of it. When I do, instantly I have a huge shift in my experience and abilities. Now I can dance. Although, this new experience may frighten me because it's unfamiliar, and I have lived so long attached to the doorknob I am likely to go back and grab it again. But over time, because now I know that I'm doing it, I can proceed to let it go for good.

What are your repeated characteristic dispositions? I am suggesting that these patterns are probably trying to resolve or manage some existential assumption you have. The problem with this lifelong effort—the self-agenda—is that no strategy can resolve it because this root exists *within*, not *without*!

This domain of mind might seem challenging to grasp, but it's best not to think of the domain of existential assumptions or bottom-line beliefs as inaccessible. They are not elsewhere, they are within your experience as it is. They just may be unseen because your attention doesn't go there. It's a mistake to hold any investigation into what's true as inaccessible. That just means you're holding that it's somehow elsewhere, and I keep asserting that's a mistake. Just because something is unseen, overlooked, or not recognized doesn't mean that it doesn't contribute significantly to your present experience. Since it's built-in to your present experience it is accessible.

Contemplation is needed to uncover these more deep-seated ideations.*

TRANSCENDING YOUR SELF-AGENDA

Sometimes we experience patterns of reactions and behavior that we desire to change. We wish we could live without negative or dysfunctional behaviors and mindsets but still seem to keep engaging in them. Even without serious introspection and contemplation, many people desire to get free from negative character traits and become a better person. But this endeavor is fraught with misunderstanding and so often doomed to failure. As mentioned, I call the source of these patterns a self-agenda, and there are reasons it is difficult to transcend.

What might constitute an agenda? We've seen self-agendas showing up in relation to existential assumptions resulting in such characteristic traits as being a timid or shy person, an aggressive or overbearing person, overly intellectual and perhaps detached from overt emotions, being sneaky and devious, fretting and worrying all the time, being sullen or grumpy, being frequently depressed, being energetic and adventurous, being nice and friendly to everyone, being superior or arrogant,

*For more about the matrix of uncognized mind, where this form of conceptual-activity resides, see the trilogy of *The Book of Not Knowing*, *Pursuing Consciousness*, and *The Genius of Being*, and find the relevant sections.

and on and on. I've gone through lists of possible examples a few times now but can't list them all. If you don't find yourself relating to anything listed so far, consider what you are characteristically bound to as a personal disposition and add it to the list.

Some of these may give you pause since they sound like positive characteristics, and how can positive patterns be an agenda? But consider, how can they not? Certainly, someone can be energetic or friendly as a norm and not as an agenda goal. But most often these drives are trying to accomplish something hidden—avoid inner pain, be liked and so accepted, feel safe, or whatever. These will be founded on an incomplete sense of self fueling an attempt to fix what's wrong.

Such things may be hard for most people to recognize. So to create a contrast to better see how these traits show up and why, imagine being without any particular self-experience—without emotions, thought patterns, ideals, drives, pursuits, ego, and whatnot. From this base, empty of most of what makes up a self-experience, you can better see commonplace human characteristics. Grasping the possibility of freedom from being bound to such unconscious drives creates the idea that you could and perhaps should transcend character traits. But let's look more closely at what we're talking about. We should separate damaging ideals from real possibilities.

We see in myths such as Jesus or Buddha, or in the psychological ideal of an actualized person, or in the personal growth aspirations of being a complete human, and in other spiritual or human growth belief systems, the idea that one can, and perhaps should, have no flaws or binding character traits. But we should consider if this possibility is actually real and attainable or just a myth and ideal.

We have no access to what was true of legends. Jesus and Buddha may have had personal struggles that we know nothing about, or they may have managed to set such things aside—by reputation they seem impressive, whatever was true. But ideals and myths are not to be trusted or considered attainable or that they should be attainable. Especially since whenever such stories become a religion, the religion will always rewrite and clean up anything that doesn't fit the image they want. They will also invent and add stuff that never occurred. With the psychological and spiritual possibilities mentioned above, we have only theories and beliefs, not a reality that is experienced as lived.

But the possibility of transcending a trait also appears to show up in others when we encounter someone who is free of a trait to which we are bound. For example, if we are shy we may be impressed with someone who is clearly not shy. This suggests that shyness is not necessary for life and is actually an impediment. It also tends to reinforce the notion that we are wrong for being so.

We see the possibility of transcendence in this case because we see someone living powerfully without this trait. But perhaps we miss the fact that the other person's challenges simply lie elsewhere. When we look carefully we will likely find they also have challenges and struggles and perhaps they have some we don't. So differences between people is not evidence that anyone can or does transcend all character traits or even all personal weaknesses or flaws.

Have you ever met anyone that is completely free and without any personal challenges? Of course not. Why do you think that is? Perhaps because it is not something that occurs. Character traits are not an option. Every person will have ways of relating to life that form patterns, which will become traits.

When we imagine the purest person, such as Buddha, even then we will see a character. For us this might appear in our imagination as calm and present, nonjudgmental and compassionate. These are character traits, but the imagined traits of legends shouldn't be trusted as true; he very likely had other traits that we know nothing about. As well there may be some guru-type that seems to be saintly and without personal challenges, and they may have achieved some measure of human composure or mind control, but their "perfection" is an act. If you followed them into their personal lives, you'd find they are not as you think and have their own challenges and foibles.

Instead of struggling to become perfect or trying to transcend your personality and character, perhaps a more effective way to go is to become deeply conscious of what you are and aren't. What's true is you really aren't your personality or traits. So in that sense no matter what traits you have, they are already transcended, so to speak, simply by becoming directly conscious and realizing that they are actually not you.

But then you have to go further and identify yourself *as* your true nature and see your person as just something you are doing, even though you are responsible for the doing. In this way, you experience yourself as distinct from your own character and from there can also change this character, because it isn't you. The following story by Sufi Nasruddin beautifully points to this consciousness.

> *How are you?*
> *Perfect, thank you. I'm traveling incognito.*
> *Oh? As what are you disguised?*
> *I am disguised as myself.*
> *Don't be silly. That's no disguise. That's what you are.*
> *On the contrary, it must be a very good disguise, for I*
> *see it has fooled you completely.*
>   SUFI MULLAH NASRUDDIN

When it comes to living life, traits and personality will still continue to function, determining the uniqueness of each person. Whatever shows as the way that person relates to life will be seen as their character or personality. So the notion of transcending one's character traits probably isn't about not having a personality or character, but about changing traits that are held as limitations or are ineffective or disempowering.

If someone indeed transcended being bound to any trait, they would be seen as different from all others. In this case, what appears would be what others see when viewing a person who fully realizes he or she is not actually a person and is without trait. Yet, for the most part, this possibility is so rare as to remain a myth.

Trying to Change

Why is trying to free yourself from your self-mind and personal traits not likely going to work? If you identified as a being that simply *had* a habit or pattern you didn't want, dropping it is possible as long as you didn't experience *being* that trait. But you do experience *being yourself* so this isn't something you can drop by an act of will. It is not a "part" of you, it is the "experience" of you. If you are not conscious of anything you are that is free of these experiences, then the only thing you have is your characteristic self. But there are overlooked layers to this experience that make change even trickier. As we saw in "Distinctions within the Self" on page 55, what you identify with determines what you experience as yourself.

You very likely experience your character traits as coming from and representing the "self behind the scenes"—what is held as the "real" you or the "source" you—from which they arise. (Recall the section about being an inner self-object in chapter 2.) Therefore, when you have the idea to transcend your character and personality, merely intellectually thinking they are not you, you will probably fail at the attempt because this is only an idea.

You have already wed your character to what you hold as the source-you and in this way identify with these traits as representing the real you. Therefore, the mere idea that they are not isn't enough to get free of them. Transcending your self is an idea that pits the notion of the source self you are *being* against the self you are actually *doing*, but this isn't seen for what it is.

If what you identify as being yourself struggles to get free of the traits arising from this same self, you will fail since you will end up with yourself no matter who wins that battle. You will be struggling against your own impulses, probably without changing the fundamental perspective from which these impulses arise. This becomes a losing battle—the snake biting its own tail. Still, what is it that you're struggling with and what are you trying to transcend?

As an analogy, consider that over time developing your character and personality was like building something out of Legos. When a child plays with such toys, each child builds their own structure, which appears different from the others. Like Legos, the kinds of traits available to humans are pretty much the same for everyone, but which ones are chosen and how they are arranged determines each unique individual. When it comes to your character traits and personality, however, one thing to get is that this structure is just serving a purpose (your individual self-survival), but it is not what you actually are—in this analogy you'd be more like the child, not the Lego structure.

If you grasp your true nature you will immediately grasp that having a personality is not the same as what you are. At some point, you may also realize that these traits have arisen and continue to arise to serve a purpose. They don't simply exist on their own or exist *as* you— even though they seem to represent you.

There is a difference between the existence of something as itself and an activity generated to serve a purpose. Anything arising merely to serve a purpose is an activity that comes and goes—it is not existentially real. In this case, the purpose for developing a "person" comprised of character traits is to create ways to manage life and to identify with a unique individual that forms the outlines of what it is that needs to persist.

This purpose can be served in many ways. Every person's character and personality is doing just that. Even though some ways are more effective or healthy than others regarding managing life or being complete, they are all serving this same purpose. Yet the substance of this activity is the same for everyone. As in the above analogy, the Legos are the same for every child, only the shapes that are built from them are different. The substance, or the Legos themselves, are all the same. Just so, what's constructed as a self-agenda is just the chosen method as to how to navigate life. Yet the one doing the choosing is actually ultimately free from anything chosen, even though they have no choice about choosing some way to do it. When you can grasp that in this way everyone is the same, you see you aren't alone in the challenge of choosing a method that may not be the healthiest or the "best" one.

Personal Inner Struggles

In your personal struggles you will always feel alone and isolated because these struggles occur in your private internal world where you are trying to deal with or overcome personally perceived challenges. In a social context, you probably try to hide, overcome, or manage these parts of you, and this increases your sense of isolation. How could you not feel alone in your struggle with being shy, angry, arrogant, unworthy, bitter, lazy, fearful, vain, withheld, restless, or any other trait that you see as a flaw or impediment or as socially unacceptable?

If you have what you consider an unacceptable or a less than desirable trait—something you tend to keep hidden or alter when dealing with others (and even if you don't hide this trait, it still doesn't seem to serve you or promote your overall interests as a social entity)—how could you not feel inwardly isolated with it? For example, say you are shy, a form of social fear. You don't necessarily want people to know you are shy. But because you are drawn into social interactions, your behavior betrays you and you know everyone sees your shyness. Yet you don't see most others as shy and so you feel isolated and alone in this shyness, whether hidden or not.

On the other hand, you may feel inwardly shy or fearful, unsure of yourself, but you hide this and project an outward sense of bravado. Again, you can see you will also feel alone with this struggle because it is kept hidden within. In different ways, with whatever self-characteristic you consider a "flaw," weakness, or unacceptable in some way, you'll tend to feel alone. The very nature of this dynamic tends to isolate you within an internal struggle.

But consider, every person struggles with this same dynamic. In this way, you are not alone but share this same feature with pretty much every person on the planet. You really needn't hide such challenges, but if you do, you can still know that the others you interact with all have their own struggles and they also feel alone with them. Knowing that you are not alone or unusual in having limiting or ineffective traits helps you accept them and also get that the person you are isn't really broken but in essence is doing the same thing everyone else is doing, albeit perhaps in a different way. In the end, it really doesn't matter; it's like various colors, everyone has a color (character) but it is really not important what it is.

What generates an ineffective trait? No characteristic trait arises without an assumed concept about yourself or about life or others that you hold as true and real. This concept is a thought, but it is held as if it is an existential reality. Can you see what concepts produce arrogance, shyness, anger, restlessness, vanity, unworthiness, and so on? Take a look at some less than sterling trait you have—even if you resist or deny that you have it—and ask yourself what is it you actually think is true about you that generates that reality? Keep focused on it until you get that it is a concept, something you are doing.

Patterns of impulses and behaviors to which you are bound that seem unwanted form an agenda that dictates what you will pursue and how you will go about trying to resolve what feels incomplete in you. Conceptual underpinnings—as mentioned in the previous sections— often go unnoticed or are just taken for granted but generate this activity in you. When you try to take on some notion of transcending your flaws or unacceptable feelings and actions, you may look toward the ideal of being a perfect human. This is not the most fruitful way to go about any such change.

Joining Your Agenda

The first thing I recommend for transcending your self-agenda is to stop resisting your own impulses and traits, if you are. Instead, accept and study them. I'm not suggesting succumbing to and mindlessly acting them out, but to accept their reality and presence fully, and join with them so you can genuinely experience them for what they are.

As you merge with and soak in these impulses and traits, you will begin to create an experience of owning them and wanting them— because you do want them, even if it seems like you don't. Once you can accept what is going on and experience that you are *doing* them, you will immediately also have an experience that you are not these very same traits.

That's because as you experience doing them you experience being at the source of the doing and so will recognize you can't *be* them. When you grasp that the very concepts that you assume to be true are what generate your particular dispositions and behaviors, this shows you they are something you are doing, allowing you a choice in the doing. For example, instead of *being* shy you are just a being *doing* shy, and therefore can also *not* do it.

This goes a long way toward grasping those traits are not you. They are concepts that you've adopted and identify with—along with the resultant impulses and activities that arise from them. To be clear, such concepts don't show up as concepts, they seem to be solid aspects of your self-experience, and so it takes some serious confrontation to grasp them for what they are. Yet when you experience them for what they are, in a way, you've already transcended them because they are no longer seen as aspects of who you really are. Instead, you experience them as concepts you are having. You will do *something* to relate to life, but it doesn't have to be that something, and you don't have to identify with being *that* way.

Once you isolate the concept that produces a trait, you can stop harboring that thought. Freed from being bound to them you can also let them go, or at least significantly reduce the power they have over you and relate to them differently. This then changes your character and personality to some degree, and that could be called genuine movement toward transcending your self-agenda.

> *The true value of a human being can be found in the degree to which he has attained liberation from the self.*
> ALBERT EINSTEIN

SUFFERING CAUSATION "RELIGION"

Let's press on to consider another dynamic that goes overlooked in people's lives but has a big impact on their perspective on life. This dynamic applies to an overlooked mental activity about the cause of lifelong suffering. Grasping this overarching dynamic, we have a better handle on how this kind of thing applies to our experience of life and what needs to be transcended to get free of it.

People have a story and explanation as to why their recurring or constant pain and suffering occurs. Remember, this suffering encompasses a large range of possibilities, including distress, dissatisfaction, irritation, upset, moods, and so on. About the cause of their suffering, they cling to this view and explanation like a religion, unquestioned. Yet this dynamic is virtually unknown for what it is.

When you are in distress or unhappy, you will attribute some cause to this dis-ease. Imagine that no matter what the "cause" is, it is simply a fabrication of mind you have made up. Most people can't see it. They think their lifelong suffering is because of such and such. But if that were true then when such and such was managed or changed, the suffering would go away for all time. But notice it doesn't.

Of course, there is suffering that is circumstantial. You get a thorn in your foot, it hurts, you remove it, and it feels better. So we think all suffering is this way. But the lifelong suffering and distress I'm referring to is rarely circumstantially derived. If it is, change the circumstance! (But pay attention, after the circumstances change, does the suffering eventually work its way back in?)

More often, however, some sense of pain, dissatisfaction, or distress seems to accompany you no matter where you go or what you do—save for occasional distractions—and is a kind of suffering that tends to be characteristic in your life. About this, you have a story as to why you are in such a pickle. Consider that this story is just a fabrication and not really why you are in distress. It is only your blind faith that assumes this is a reality, and the story is always biased and myopic and based on your, usually unconscious, reasons for choosing it.

Let's look at some simplistic examples to draw out this distinction. Someone might live life with the attitude that life never gave them a break. This is not true. But they think it is. They live as if the world is somehow against them and takes every opportunity to screw them over. They designate this as the cause of their suffering. But I guarantee it is not. Their own perspective and thinking and actions have created their distress, not anything circumstantial, even if bad things have happened from time to time.

Perhaps someone lives life in a desperate search for distractions, unknowingly attributing the cause of their depressive states to a boring life that will plunge them into despair unless some adventure or project keeps their attention occupied. Again, they fail to realize the source of their despair is within their own mind and has nothing to do with life circumstance—which is just a distraction to keep the mind from confronting what's there without such distraction.

Another possible scenario might be thinking "no one loves me, I am alone and the fault lies in the callousness of others. I suffer this condition because of them." Again, is this true? Not a chance. No matter how callous or caring others are, the pain is created by you, not circumstance.

Someone with mental challenges of some kind imagines that their pain and suffering is caused by other people slipping into craziness around them; over time it becomes intolerable to live with those people and they must move on, resistant as they are. But the situation just repeats itself as time goes by. This is because the problem lies within their own mind, not on any circumstance.

Some common supposed causes of discontent might show up as, I'm not beautiful enough, I wasn't given the right intelligence or education, the world is not smart enough to understand me, I'm better than others and they lack the qualities I need to stimulate me and make me happy, others are prejudiced against me, I'm just naturally angry because the world is asinine, I don't get enough love and understanding, I'm not good enough, everyone else is better than me, the world doesn't give me everything I deserve.

These might be rather simplistic and superficial examples, others might seem rather bland or as if based on more common sense, but it gives you a starting place to consider. There is no way to come close to describing every possible scenario people come up with to explain their unease. You have to discover what your particular suffering causation "religion" is and then make a leap in consciousness to grasp that it is all conceptually produced.

I call it "religion" because it has the same power as blind belief—in this case, believing that the world is such and such a way and the solution would be to attain another circumstance or personal condition. But this doesn't consider that the view is made up. It also doesn't take into account the fact that the supposed resolution never happens, and this failure is always blamed on a cause that isn't really the cause.

The whole domain of unrecognized existential assumptions and bottom-line motivations, as well as agenda strategies, will have a lot to do with this perspective—as we touched on earlier. Whatever your beliefs are they will dominate your perspective and relating and influence your actions and behavior. To get free, it is essential to get what this dynamic is for you, realize it is a concept you are making up, and drop it.

SUGGESTIONS FOR CONTEMPLATION
Cause of Suffering

When you recall your history, you'll likely find good times and bad, but overall, what is your sense of yourself and life, your constant and solid perspective and personal experience? This may be difficult to grasp, especially if you haven't experienced some serious freedom from your very person. But consider, in your experience, your perspective isn't nothing, or neutral, or open. So what is it? What is your characteristic way of being? Generally, what emotional-mood-attitude disposition is characteristic and common for you?

Are you generally grumpy or angry, carefree or whimsical, fearful or shy, self-pitying or a victim, forceful or controlling, gullible or naive, dull or stupid, self-centered or arrogant, distant or aloof, friendly or engaging, worried or nervous, intellectual or what? What is your personal experience of being you in life? Be honest about it.

Within that experience is likely some constant aspect that isn't free, isn't happy or complete. What do you think causes you to be that way? What is your story about the cause of this characteristic sense of discomfort?

What story do you tell yourself is behind you being the way you are and life being the way it is?

It's good to get that this is just a story. You cause your suffering in this way, but actually the story itself doesn't cause it. Your mind does through the created ideations that the story is based upon. Now, can you isolate the ideation(s)—the assumed concepts—that generate this overall sense of lack or unease? Do you have a sense of the cause of your overall feeling of being incomplete, being stuck the way you are, or life being the way it is?

We see that the domain of beliefs has a strong influence on our experience. Since beliefs are usually just "lived from" rather than inspected, it can be difficult to see their real influence. Can you find what I'm calling this causation "religion"? It can be tricky.

The religion of the future will be a cosmic religion. It will transcend a personal God and avoid dogma and theology.
ALBERT EINSTEIN

Beyond any one contribution to the drama of life is an array of contributing factors. We don't really need to go into every single belief, concept, assumption, or perspective to know that life is full of tons of drama regardless of source. What drives us is obviously pain and pleasure, suffering and ecstasy, comfort and discomfort. These are the basic dynamics of life, founded on the principle of survival. Within these dynamics our struggle often has both strife and promise, but what is behind it all? As Shakespeare contributed, although it seems full of sound and fury, it really signifies nothing (*Macbeth*, act 5, scene 5).

MORE ON IMPULSES AND DRIVES

The Pee Analogy

Have you ever been desperate to pee? Then you finally get to a place where you can let go—Ahhh! What a relief! Joy! Yet the pleasure of peeing is really a relief from the suffering driving you to do it. Can you get that?

The thing is, all of life is that way. Consider that life has general and specific forces constantly pressing on you. This creates a form of suffering that is rather constant. You take action to relieve this distress in various ways. When you manage to relieve yourself it seems like pleasure, but can you see how it relates to the suffering? Pleasure and pain are two sides of the same coin. If you are in distress in some way, relieving this pain feels like pleasure. How many pleasurable experiences and circumstances can you identify that have their root in getting out of suffering?

Normally you don't notice you are constantly breathing. But if you stop breathing, pressure builds up to force you to breathe. This pressure reads out as increasing discomfort, and when you finally breathe it feels good, doesn't it? Even now without holding your breath, when you put attention on breathing you might think it feels good to breathe. Yet notice that it fades into the background when you once again take it for granted.

Can you find any pleasure that in some way doesn't relate to suffering? It seems I'm making an argument that pleasure is based on pain. I'm not. The argument is that they are inseparable. But why can't pleasure be the natural state all by itself?

Why would it? Life is about survival, not feeling good. The only reason pursuing feeling good is your goal, once again, is because feeling good indicates that your well-being—on whatever level and in whatever way it is occurring—is going your way. In other words, your interpretation of circumstance or your state of being is that your survival—mental, emotional, physical—is working out. If not, you suffer, and this acts as motivation to attempt to bring your state back to some sort of positive. This positive sense suggests you are being effective in life, that everything is OK. Can you see the dynamic I'm suggesting here?

Again, as we discovered in part 2, "Getting Free from Unnecessary Suffering," only when you imagine some other experience is better than the one you're having does the one you are having become painful. Remember, you could also imagine an experience that is far worse than what you're having and then your current experience would be seen as pleasant or good. Can you see the different disposition and state that arises when you do one or the other? Dramatic difference, isn't it? Notice once again that this is all created via concept and imagination, not real life.

As we see, positive and negative determine each other. I'd like to make a distinction, however, between something I'll call "bliss"—just a term I'm using to refer to a different state than normal—and pleasure. Pleasure is about feeling good and positive and occurs in contrast to suffering or pain. Bliss, on the other hand, is about freedom—freedom from being bound to or dominated by either pain or pleasure. In this way, we might say bliss could be a natural state and yet is rarely experienced because self-survival, our real commitment, overwhelms our experience with its demands—none of which are freedom.

Love and Each Other

In opposition to suffering, we like pleasure or positive emotions. Yet if pleasure is related to pain we see it isn't an isolated matter. But what experience do we like most? Love seems about the most positive and favored emotion. So just for fun, let's look into love a bit.

Out of all the emotions people have, most hold love to be perhaps the most positive feeling. Everyone seems to love love. Yet such a feeling-disposition is often rarer than we would like. If we like it so much why not produce it more? Obviously because we don't hold that it's in our hands but caused by outside forces. This being the case, we must wait until someone lovable comes into our sphere of awareness. Yet what makes someone lovable?

We do, of course. We decide what makes someone acceptable or not, and once accepted they can then be loved if the prerequisites are met. The "prerequisites" or mental connections that brings someone into the domain of lovable, again, may seem out of our hands. Yet it is our brains that make the connection. With such popularity, however, why do we have so few interpretations of love? This connection serves a purpose, as do all interpretations and emotions. So what is that purpose?

Before considering this purpose, perhaps we should distinguish between love and *need* so we can focus on the right experience. Many of the impulses that pass for loving someone are actually emotionally and psychologically needing someone—some feeling of dependency. Such need or dependency is not love, it is actually a self-serving and self-referencing impulse. When we feel like we need someone—that having a particular relationship with another is essential for our emotional well-being—this suggests a need or dependency, not love, even if we also have some form of love. Emotional desperation or need is obviously due to some psychological lack within oneself.

When children say they love their parents, what are they saying? Their lives and survival, even in a physical sense, depend on the parents. So is that emotion a need—perhaps dependency—or is it love? It is a difficult question, isn't it?

We want to think that our children love us, but why would that be true? How would they create such an emotion of caring for our well-being except as it relates to their well-being? Do they have the capacity to consider the parent beyond their own needs? Perhaps, but it also may be true that they don't. Instead, they may feel need rather than love and have been trained to call it love. On the other hand, perhaps as a relatively unformed and unsophisticated being they may be open enough to feel love just because they appreciate the wonder of another. Hard to say. Perhaps it is a combination of both.

As adults, how much of our "loving" emotions are actually need? Again, we should make a distinction between emotional dependency and what we think of as love. If we feel there is a lack within us that drives us in our relationships, this is a different activity. Having someone fill this lack isn't an act of love. What good does that do the other? None really. It isn't designed with them in mind except how they can serve our needs. Do you see the difference?

It seems love is about accepting another, connecting with them, and wishing them well. Need is about you. Of course, this need often shows up in the domain of romantic love but can also be seen in family dynamics and other forms of human contact. Love, on the other hand, is about the well-being of the other—even if it also fulfills us in some way.

What is the outcome of feeling love? We feel a strong connection with and desire to care for another like we would ourselves; they become something of an extension of self. So the evolution of love may have something to do with creating close alliances between people so that we serve the interests of each other and increase the chances of survival to the benefit of all. It appears this might be its purpose.

We may feel good when we feel love, but it goes beyond feeling good. It shows up in actions—protecting, nurturing, supporting, helping, giving, and so on. These actions go both ways if the love goes both ways. Of course, the flip side is the anguish of losing a loving relationship as the benefits of physical and emotional partnership and connection evaporate. Such a broken alliance seems to toss us back into an isolated self, surviving on its own, and this isolated self-experience in contrast to the experience of selves-in-union usually feels bad. This appears to be the cost of love lost.

We aren't just talking of romance, but all shades and degrees of love. For example, in times past the word was used more freely to show alliance or unity with others—perhaps to show acceptance and approval, absent of much emotion other than feelings of good will. Such use of the word expands our field of love quite a bit. Beyond expanding it, how can we make it more abundant and perhaps commonplace?

After living with an ambition to view a perfect cherry blossom in the movie *The Last Samurai*, on the battlefield our dying hero looks up one last time to see the wind blowing dozens of cherry blossoms and says, "Perfect. They're *all* perfect!" Recognizing the inherent perfection of everyone would go a long way toward accepting others, thus narrowing the gap between encountering them and loving them.

As suggested, our first requisite seems to be to find someone as acceptable. If we allow everyone and everything to be perfectly what and how they are, we accomplish this first step. Once we accept someone, we're closer to loving them because we allow them to exist "as is," and that reduces or eliminates our resistance to them or fear of them. If we also make a leap to hold that they are in some way the same as us, or that our selves are all versions of the same self, or some other similar shift in perspective, there is little standing in the way of loving others.

We need to guard against founding such goals on ideals or fantasies, however. Our loving disposition will obviously set the stage for our relating, but this shouldn't be seen as demanding any particular kind of behavior on our part other than that it's motivated by a state of love or compassion rather than other impulses. It doesn't have to "look" loving, it simply has to be that.

I know this is easier said than done. I'm simply looking into the matter and opining as to what I see. I am aware that there are so many emotional and mental forces acting on each of us that a muddle of feelings may overwhelm any good intentions to the contrary. Even so, we can sort out the various emotional activities that dominate our experience and move in a different direction if we're up for the challenge.

But we'd need to include all of our emotions in this effort, and the love we undertake likely can't be reduced to one feeling, or even *a* feeling. I would suspect that in trying to make love a central motivating factor, it would have to be an ingredient within all our various experiences and so influence all of our emotional states. This is suggesting that love would show up differently than the particular feeling we call love.

Rather than a particular emotion, we'd find love to be a principle or open experience that influences our other emotions as well. This principle and experience would then manifest in some way even within our negative feelings, without interfering with or suppressing such feelings. A new idea perhaps, but an interesting possibility, especially because in this way we could go beyond simplistic fantasies and ideals of what it would look like to be always loving, to create a real and grounded experience that changes our normal life perspective. Maybe not easily attainable but a possible direction in which to consider moving.

At this point, we are considering love beyond emotion. Some state or "perspective" that embodies a principle that isn't bound to an emotion but to a disposition that isn't personal or based upon our needs or even how we feel. This is an unusual proposition for humans because our experience is designed around a self-survival that is wed to managing life primarily via distinct drives, impulses, and feeling-states.

Instead of restricting ourselves to an emotion, we can expand our consideration of love to that of something we might call compassion—since I don't think we've created a word yet for what I'm considering here. Compassion also relates to others, wishing them well and taking action to empower them, but this doesn't have to show up as an emotion. We tend to think that every impulse that motivates us must have a clear and dominant positive or negative charge that is often emotional in nature. But in our new distinction, consider that compassion itself requires no emotion. It only requires the activation of the principle that is compassion and applying it to our thinking, actions, and interactions so that it dominates our experience and intent and influences our feeling-sense and perspective.

I don't think attempting such a shift should be seen as being a "good" or morally superior person, but instead considered because we grasp that it is actually an effective way of relating and an empowering experience to have. I'm not at all suggesting that we always be positive, polite, or kind—but that our actions are motivated by an impersonal yet inclusive impulse that serves or benefits others, not just ourselves. Therefore, such compassion may appear confrontational or even ruthless sometimes, as well as kind. But in either case, it is founded on the intent to empower or benefit everyone involved.

It is difficult for us to imagine doing what's best or empowering for another without having some motivating emotion or agenda behind it. It's also hard for us to imagine being a compassionate person without all the trappings of looking like a "good" person. But such impersonal compassion isn't solely based on one's self. It's being willing to serve others whether they know you're doing that or not, to act to improve their lives or increase their consciousness no matter how they feel about it or about you. So the impulse is of a different nature than most of our impulses.

It may be a bit like being motivated to "do the right thing" even though it doesn't serve you personally. This might be because you're committed to a larger principle that goes beyond personal agenda and if you didn't do the "right thing," you would violate this principle and so generate an intolerable experience. As Louis Armstrong once said, "I don't let my mouth say anything my heart can't stand."

Another example, although an unlikely one, would be: If you could save all of humanity yet in so doing you would have to die, what would you do? Probably save humanity, because you also identify with "us" and couldn't stand the pain of letting everyone else die.

Of course, what we are addressing here is of a different nature, but these examples may provide touchstones to help us consider how we could be motivated to take action that isn't seen as exclusively self-serving. If we realize that compassion *for* all of us is actually empowering *to* all of us, including ourselves, it provides enough motivation to pursue it.

> *When we are no longer able to change a situation,*
> *we are challenged to change ourselves.*
>
> VIKTOR FRANKL

PART IV

❧

New Perspectives and Powerful Distinctions That Change Experience

We completed the work of ending unnecessary suffering in part 2. Since now we'll have so much time on our hands—being free from all that suffering—perhaps learning to create more powerful experiences can fill that vacuum. This work can now more successfully be tackled because our previous studies have laid a powerful foundation for increased breakthroughs, transformations, and a deeper consciousness.

Having learned new skills in investigating and controlling your mind, you can now enter a rather advanced level of study and tackle newly crafted experiences that can further change your life. There are principles that once adopted make a huge difference in one's experience. Perhaps touching on some of these would be useful for you if you're interested in changing your experience into a more powerful, effective, and perhaps less stressful one.

In order to give these principles the best chance at being effective, however, it's good to not only see them as practical and attainable, but also base them on your understanding of how such experiences are created. Although the existential nature of how experience is created is another study, which can be gleaned in some of my other books, what's also true is you don't really need to know any of that for these principles to work. You just need to adopt them. But the more you can grasp what they are and how they work, the stronger their influence will be.

You should also consider how any of these distinctions fit with or relate to your social structure and how they might contribute to healthier mental-emotional states. As seen, mental-emotional states play an all-important role in your experience of life. Certainly, you can entertain abstract philosophical notions or spiritual aspirations that imply a freedom from the binding force of your mind and emotions, but life as you live it usually tells another story. When you consider changing your experience by adopting new principles to live by, it's best to also include how they relate to your emotions because in order for these principles to be active in your daily experience they must be applied to life as it's lived, not just life as it's imagined.

Generating new distinctions is how we change our experience. Some of what's to come will likely to be new distinctions for you, and others have already been addressed in some form in previous books, but I want to expand on them here.

CHAPTER EIGHT

Creating New Experiential Abilities

INVESTIGATING EXISTENTIALLY

Earlier I touched on the domain I call existential thinking. This kind of approach is useful for experientially grasping the upcoming assertions. You can hear about them and understand the basic ideas, but this will not change your experience. Unless you can experience the principle operating within your own perceptions, mind, and emotions, it won't change anything. To know them intimately and to fully experience them you need to delve into them existentially.

Toward that end, as you consider each principle, ask questions such as: What is it really? How does it come to pass? What is its purpose? What is it doing? How does it work? These questions point you in the direction of experiencing the nature of its existence.

I suspect that most people look at existential thinking—or existential anything—as pretty much an intellectual or philosophical pursuit and wonder what such academic activity has to do with genuine experience. This is a misunderstanding of what I mean by existential. To grasp the existence of something—its existential nature—is experiential. If it's not experiential, then it's not existential.

Grasping the nature, composition, components, and specific realities of each distinction or principle to be discussed can only occur within our experience and will change how we perceive that subject. This is the domain of an existential investigation, the activity of approaching a subject to grasp its real nature. This is experiential, not just intellectual. It is important to consider the following distinctions and principles in that light.

For example, if you go back to our work on suffering, notice the difference between hearing and understanding intellectually what's said about dissatisfaction, depression, or whatever, and being inside of that malaise and experientially grasping what's going on rather than just being at the effect of its presence. As you can see by now, most people can't do this because they don't make a distinction between hearing or thinking about something and experiencing its reality.

If we don't know *that* or *how* we can experience the components— what makes up a particular experience so it can exist at all—or experience the existential nature of that experience, we are hampered in successfully adopting it. We are stuck simply being at the effect of whatever is perceived. Leaping beyond this "stuckness" is obtained through existentially investigating the matter and getting what an experience really is. In so doing, we can now successfully make a new distinction or adopt a principle and make it real. In this way, it alters our experience. All of these new distinctions and principles are conceptual-actions that enhance life.

COMPLETION

Our first new distinction is called "completion" or "completing" something. We have looked at being complete and, although they are related, they are not the same. Being complete is a state or condition. Completion is an ability.

There are various ways to approach or create the distinction of completion. To "complete" something in this context means you experience the subject matter as itself (in the normal sense of those words and not the direct consciousness way I often use that term) and only itself, without attachments or residual conceptual-activities influencing your experience of it. Again, see our work on suffering for lots of examples of how concepts influence experience.

This basic ability involves freeing one's experience from dispositions built on all sorts of self-serving complications. It eliminates reactions and attachments that are unnecessary and ineffective for producing a healthy, open, and free experience. Whatever the subject, the goal is to experience it as completely that, and only that.

These statements point to its social function and benefit, but that doesn't tell you much about the principle itself. In order to get at the principle, we need to know something about how our perceptive-experience normally arises. As we've seen, whenever we perceive something—an object, a feeling, an action, a statement, a person, and so on—we automatically assess this thing in relation to our self-concerns, history, and beliefs. This adds a great deal to it.

To "complete" something is to take off all the additional interpretations and associations that relate that something to our personal agenda and self-concerns so that it is completely or only the thing it is without those additions. We are not prone to do this because relating everything to ourselves is automatic and seems like a necessary component for our self-preservation and life management.

As we saw with unnecessary suffering, simply stopping the activity of mind that creates distress allows us to experience what's there more as it is. When we remove this conceptual addition, we see more clearly. But in this distinction, completion goes beyond interrupting automatic imaginings.

Our personal history creates the context for relating to any particular thing. We'll likely also have a history of previous dealings with whatever we are encountering or with similar subjects. We associate the past with every encounter we have and this influences our perception and expectations in relation to it.

We also apply meaning to whatever we perceive—what it means culturally, what it means in this context and at this time, and what it means to us personally—and we compare this subject to our assessment of ourselves, our strengths and weaknesses, our self-judgments, and so on. The good or bad of it only occurs through relating *it* to *us*.

All of these additions to the subject determine most of our experience of it and so our reactions to it. These added activities may result in an overwhelming emotion or simply influence our disposition. Yet such reactions determine our experience and relationship to the thing. If we eliminate these automatic additional conceptual-activities we will also eliminate their influence on our experience and our reactions to this influence. Yet how is this done?

The first thing we need to do is make a distinction between our experience of the subject without relating it to our self-concerns, and our experience of it after such relating. The essential task of "completing" something is to experience it free from our automatic self-serving influences, such as our self-agenda, self-concerns, and our history. To complete something means our experience of that something is completely and only what it is—for example, if it is gold then it is purely and only gold; it is not gold with copper or value or desire or anything else added to it.

Although completion is not the same activity, it is consistent with the principle of experiencing something "for itself" rather than "for me." Using this "for itself" ability provides the foundation for completion by allowing us to shift how we experience something. Yet there is a difference between perceiving something for itself and completion.

The ability to perceive something for itself is to subtract all meaning, judgment, labels, charge, function, history, and the like—all that occurs by relating it to ourselves—so we can perceive it as simply *that*, an object, a feeling, a concept, an entity, or whatever. Although this is a powerful ability, still we can't manage life within this possibility. You couldn't survive if you only perceived everything for itself because you'd have no way to know how to navigate life—there would be no function, history, meaning, use, value, positive or negative, and so on.

Although that may provide temporary relief from the burdens imposed by survival, you couldn't maintain your life if you only perceived everything for itself. Taken to extreme, you wouldn't know what to eat, how to take care of yourself or use a tool, assess the validity of something, and so on. So to survive you must create some activity that will allow you to do those things, but without all the clutter that usually just bogs down the works in unnecessary conceptual additions. Completion bridges this gap.

We use the "for itself" ability to strip away unnecessary activities like judgment, past challenges, projections, expectations, and so forth to create an experience of something in present time, freed of these activities that influence our experience too much and often in disempowering ways. This shift needs to be done independent of any reaction we might already have and free from concerns about where it might end up. Completion allows us to create freedom from reactivity based on automatically relating something to our self-concerns, but still preserve basic assessments like function, social agreements, validity, and so on.

To complete something, set aside personal wants and needs and simply see what it is without relating it to you and your needs or fears. This may seem to undermine your concerns and emotional needs, but it clears the deck of so much automatic knee-jerk reactions and influences that it allows you to see the subject free of personal bias. This will immediately create a different experience of the subject, and you can go forward from there.

For example, perhaps you notice you're uncomfortable around Bob. With pretty much everything he says and does, you feel less than and vulnerable and are immediately on the defensive. You notice your experience changes simply when he enters the room. This is all undoubtedly based on a history of relating to Bob and from your own self-view and self-esteem causing you to see what Bob says as dangerous and hurtful to your sense of value. Due to your low self-esteem, you think Bob sees you as worthless and you feel incapable of withstanding his view because you unconsciously think the same thing about yourself. From such a perspective, reactions are pretty much inevitable.

So to complete your experience of Bob you need to see him as simply a person in this moment, without the domination of history and independent from your self-concerns. Although this is actually easier done than said, the strength of these automatic survival activities can make it pretty difficult to do—especially in such an extreme scenario as above. You may be able to do this in a moment or it might take you a bit of time to shift your brain and perceptions to see him this way. Once you can see him as just "that," a person for himself and as himself, without the past interpretive add-ons, you will find you don't have any of your previous reactions. This is because your experience of him is complete by seeing him as just a person, newly and in present time. He is now a rather new experience and you can relate to him quite differently.

When you complete your experience of Bob, everything he says or does is simply what he says or does. It is about him, NOT about you! You see him through the lens of how he affects himself, not how he affects you. For example, if he is angry at you, you aren't upset with his anger; instead you see the pain in him and the suffering he experiences as a result of being angry. You are more likely to experience sympathy for him than to react defensively against his behavior. In a sense, you see it as his problem, not yours.

When you are complete there is no unfinished business left in your experience, nothing reactive or in need of attention to correct or manage. If you feel off somehow or as if you need to "do" something to manage or alter your experience, it is not complete. You are not having an experience that is really about present time. Something is unsettled or disturbed in some way. When you are complete you are simply present and without disturbance or reactivity in regard to the subject.

When I was a child living in Singapore, I caught a tropical disease. I was given all sorts of things as a cure but the main thing was a purple pill I had to take. This purple pill caused a lot of pain in my body, and so mind. Since I had to take it daily for quite some time, I developed a real aversion to that pill. Much later as an adult I noticed I hated the color purple. Investigating this uncalled-for reaction, I rediscovered the trauma of the purple pill from my past. I consciously set out to disengage the pill and its unpleasant effects from the color purple and managed to free purple from my aversion. Now I can even enjoy the color purple (sometimes).

This is a small example of freeing experience from a past association. But there are many such associations and connections that create an "incomplete" experience. Completing something means bringing it back to a simple and present experience free of all kinds of unnecessary and inappropriate additions that burden your awareness of it.

This can be done with any emotion, belief, idea, object, person, and so on. An emotion is simply that feeling—it is not motivation, negative or positive. A belief is only a belief—a concept that something is true without knowing what is actually true. An object is just an object, not its name, its usefulness, concepts about it, and so on. Can you see the direction in which to go to create this ability?

If, after you experience being complete, you want to re-establish your reactive relationship to something, there is nothing preventing you. On the other hand, once freed of this reactive force the new experience is most often seen as so much better and freer than the previous self-referencing reactivity that you have no desire to re-create your former form of suffering.

Also, from here you can consciously create a new relationship to the subject, at least temporarily, rather than remain trapped in old patterns. The result of completing something in this way is an increased sense of freedom and balance. This occurs as you shift mentally and emotionally to "standing on your own experiential feet" as opposed to being pressed this way or that by automatic self-generated reactions to whatever is encountered. Consider developing this ability and what it might contribute to your experience of life.

TURNING-INTO

A good portion of our experience includes feeling-sensations, some of which we wish we didn't have. We attach meaning and a positive or negative charge to each sensation that comes our way. Some of these are unwanted and last longer than a moment. We've seen that the flow of our experience moves in an automatic and usually unconscious way. Our most common disposition to this condition is that we have no choice but to put up with and find ways to deal with these feeling-sensations. Yet there may be another possibility we've overlooked.

If we imagine that the automatic flow of feeling-experience is like a river that goes only downstream, then in this metaphor "turning-into" would be akin to turning against this flow and moving aggressively upstream. The "downstream" in this case is what occurs naturally whenever we encounter a feeling-sensation coming our way; we automatically proceed to interpret the experience, classify it as negative or positive, and react to it as is dictated by the mechanisms of our self-survival—we call this "being at the effect" of what we perceive.

Instead of following this automatic flow of experience, with turning-into we deliberately press our feeling-attention to move toward and into the incoming sensation rather than react to it. Turning-into is an experiential skill; no intellect is needed, except to understand what it is and having the will to use it.

As seen, your first impulse to any feeling is to react to whatever is encountered by automatically relating it to your self-needs and concerns. This results in a reactivity or "effect" that moves your experience away from a genuine encounter with what's there. Being at the effect of something is a personal experience that has to do with what it means to you, and this is moving your experience in the direction of you, not it. With turning-into, this direction is reversed.

Again, to be clear, turning-into is not an intellectual action and doesn't require any understanding about how or why it works to do it. It simply requires moving your feeling-attention toward any currently arising sensation—usually a negative one—and aggressively moving into it, embracing the experience rather than automatically reacting to or resisting it. In so doing, the negative feeling-experience fades or disappears.

This simple act disrupts our automatic mental-emotional and nervous system reactions. Since our knee-jerk reaction is whatever effect the subject has on us, when we set out to fully embrace and experience what's there, this reaction is short-circuited. This action demands no insight about the subject, it only requires directing feeling-attention to move into the presence of what's encountered. This is done without trying to predict what will be there and without resistance to it changing as the process of turning-into it proceeds.

For example, say you encounter a bodily pain, such as a headache. The natural first reaction is to consider it negative and resist it being there. You're likely to be upset with the pain and try to get away from it somehow. This is the normal experience of having a headache, and it hurts.

Instead, when turning-into it, you fully feel the sensation that is there, exactly where and how it is, and move your feeling-attention into it as if to embrace it, trying to fully and deeply feel every part of it—similar to what might occur if you wanted it. You don't even call it a headache; it is simply whatever feeling is there without judgment or expectation. As you keep moving in this direction, the sensation will change. As it does, simply keep moving into whatever is there. While you do this, the pain will lessen and probably disappear.

As you turn-into something, remember not to look for what you *think* is there or what *was* there. Instead, feel whatever *is* there currently, even if it changes. If it moves or slips to the side or takes different shapes or locations, go after it as it is and fully feel it. Don't let it get away or hide in any way. Go after it aggressively with your feeling-attention, even if it changes in some way—and it will tend to change. Make sure you get it all, like herding sheep; if some try to split from the group you need to surround them and include them with your engulfing feeling. This is an important point. If you back off or let it slip away or ignore the present and current form it is taking in any moment, turning-into it won't work.

Since pain is actually an activity you're doing—as are all interpretations—when you turn-into the feeling-sensation, concentrating on fully feeling it as it is, the interpretation of pain begins to disappear. Upon totally embracing and turning-into what's there, whatever would normally be generated by the mind as interpretation and reaction will dissipate because, contrary to common sense and what seems to be just an obvious observation, these don't actually exist on their own.

But you don't need to know any of this, you simply have to turn-into whatever is there. As you do, it will lessen and dissipate. If it is conceptually created it will disappear. If it is physiologically created then it will return once you stop turning-into it if that activity persists. You'll find far more is generated conceptually than you might think, even when it seems to be physically produced. In any case, that's a description of turning-into, but you have to do it to really get the idea. It's quite simple, it just takes the discipline of doing it.

COMMUNICATION

In our social world communication is the bedrock that makes it possible for us to even have what we experience as a social life. How well we communicate and how well we listen determines a great deal of how successful or satisfying our social life is. I have written about communication quite a bit in other books. Here let me touch on some of the essentials found in this invention and perhaps touch on some points that may have been overlooked.

The main thing that distinguishes real communication from what passes as the many activities done in the name of communication is what gets across, not what is done. If the communicated experience of one person is experienced by another as it is for the first person, then communication took place. Do you see the difference between that and all of the activity that takes place under the guise of communicating?

It isn't the motions or methods that determine communication. Those are only forms of language. It's what actually gets across that determines if communication has taken place or not. No matter how much talking or other activities take place that are usually called communicating, this doesn't mean communication has occurred. If one's experience is not experienced by another as it is by the first person, then communication did not take place.

Sometimes people make this harder than it needs to be, however, by looking for a complete psychic merging of experiences. Although something like that may happen with deep communication, all that really needs to occur is you grasp exactly what the other person is trying to get across, or vice versa. This can be quite simple, such as in conveying logistical information, or it might require much more empathy and perhaps lengthy dialogue to make it happen.

One principle that helps a great deal for you to successfully interact is not to respond or take action in relation to what someone is saying until you make sure you have gotten their experience the way they experience it. Once this has occurred then your response will relate to what's so for them and not just what is so for you or what you think is going on with them. This helps avoid a lot of misunderstandings, as well as the reactions that occur based on irrelevant and often mistaken notions or projections.

If you get bogged down in your own reactivity to what someone is saying, this will not allow you to hear what is actually being communicated because your attention will be on your reactions and not what is true for the other. It is highly likely that your reactions are based on what you are projecting their experience to be and then relating that to you, and so you won't be relating to their experience at all, even though you think you are. Such reactivity is not only unnecessary it is ineffective and dysfunctional.

Strange as it might sound to people, the moment you have an opinion or judgment about what the other is communicating—or what you think they are communicating—you immediately cut off true listening and connection. You will not be getting them, you will be experiencing your opinion or judgment, and those are never *them* or their experience. Can you see that?

Due to its automatic nature, it may be difficult to suspend such activity for a bit in order to really "hear" what someone is trying to get across. After all, we tend to think of our opinions and judgments as important or significant. Whether they are or not, they are *our* experience, not *theirs*, and communication demands that it be theirs. Perhaps this is a new observation for most people, but it's something to consider.

It might be difficult to accept that you are not being heard or are not really hearing another sometimes, but in order to be clear about and activate this distinction of real communication, you need to know when it is occurring and when it's not. No matter how much activity is done, if grasping or really hearing the other's experience doesn't take place then the communication has not been successful. If a communication does not get across, it is best to acknowledge this and either let it go or try again.

PURPOSE

People often want purpose in their lives. We see purpose as giving us a direction and a reason for getting up in the morning. Yet purpose is often misunderstood, and in my view, it is sometimes conflated with other motivating factors that aren't it.

There is a difference between following impulsive drives that pursue a mostly unconscious agenda and creating a purpose. It seems most of us live as if a purpose is what motivates us to do something. When following impulsive drives, however, the purpose is always self-survival, and for us this serves the self and self-agenda. Therefore, no purpose has been created; instead, survival is simply the default mode for all creatures. Let's consider purpose in a more creative way.

First, for clarity we need to make a distinction between a goal and a purpose. Goal and purpose are not the same thing. A goal is a specific result you want to attain. Purpose, on the other hand, is the reason you are engaging in an activity or pursuit or the reason for which something exists or is created.

As an example, let's say you take up running. Your purpose might be to become stronger and healthier. A goal could be to run a marathon. Working toward the goal of running a marathon is consistent with your development and purpose. Yet once you achieve this goal the purpose doesn't end but continues toward the next goal(s). See the difference?

You might say your purpose for picking up the trash along your jogging path is the same as the goal of picking up the trash. But really your purpose might be because it produces in you a better experience of your environment; in other words, it makes you happier to do so. Thus, you may also trim a branch on the path, or move rocks you or others might trip on, and so on, and these are all consistent with this same purpose.

Goals are a subset or tool of the purpose—they represent activities and aims that are either on purpose or not. If they are on purpose, they are in the process of realizing the objectives for which these activities are being done. If they are not, then they are off purpose.

So what pushes us to act or try to achieve anything if not a purpose? As mentioned, again, a distinction we should make is between being driven by our self-agenda and creating a purpose. The inherent drive and force of self-survival comes with life, as a matter of fact it creates life. I've written elsewhere about the extent of this force and activity. It applies to everything we are identified with—body, character, history, self-concept, social status, assumptions, beliefs, programming, and so on. From this complex of attachments many activities are pursued pretty much automatically—the purpose being self-survival.

We've seen that within this self-survival domain, whatever is held to be incomplete, inadequate, or in any way not what it should be, develops into a self-agenda, the pursuit of which promises to resolve all that. It doesn't matter that such a pursuit won't work, in many ways—both subtle and gross—it determines the course our lives will take and the reactions we have as we pursue trying to resolve ourselves. Many of the "goals" that arise from this pursuit become ideals we feel we must attain in order to become complete.

These self-agenda ideals are often pursued as if they form the purpose for our lives and they may seem promising and attainable at times. But in the end our efforts in this regard will fail to be realized because our "flaws" can't be remedied from any outside attainment since they exist within us not outside of us. This agenda dominates much of our life-pursuits and, along with other aspects of self-survival, produces the drives that push us to do what we do. Such drives can also be confused with having a purpose outside the default of self-survival. But they aren't.

You might wonder why I brought up the subset of a self-agenda again in this context. As I said, the activity of the self-agenda often gets confused with having a purpose in life. Don't confuse creating a purpose with having an ideal. You may have some ideas of what would be ideal to accomplish, yet these ideas may well be generated by historical programming and your agenda. They are also likely to be stuck in a form or image of how that accomplishment should look.

For example, perhaps you feel you are a lesser human being because you grew up on a poor farm and were generally looked down upon by other more well-to-do people. You might form an ideal of becoming super rich, thinking this will bring you happiness and solve your dilemma of feeling less than. Therefore, it might seem like your purpose in life is to get rich, and yet this is not a consciously created purpose, it is an unconscious drive that will not resolve your malady even if you accomplish it. If you do, you will simply be a rich person feeling less than.

Creating a purpose, on the other hand, creates the reason for your pursuit. It doesn't have to be based on anything past and shouldn't be wed to a personal agenda. Consistent with a created purpose are goals you may adopt—for yourself or agreements of goals to work toward with others. Again, this should not be confused with getting the others or the pursuit to fit some image you have of what they should look like.

Purpose does not determine how things should look or even in what manner they should unfold. Refer back to our example of the purpose of taking up running. We can see if our purpose is to become healthier, we could approach that in all sorts of ways—eating healthy foods, exercising regularly, doing t'ai chi, meditating, taking supplements, and so on—whatever we think will improve our health. Running is only one approach. The methods that arise to realize goals only need to be consistent with the purpose, not to any ideals or predetermined image you may have of what it will look like to pursue or accomplish something. When a fixed image is the goal, this inevitably stems from an ideal, not a created purpose.

The distinction here is perhaps better seen by the fact that in following an agenda we are driven by unconscious forces, whereas a purpose is created consciously and so no agenda-based ideal image will relate to it. Any created purpose for a project or a created purpose to guide one's life is created, not found or inherited. Certainly, once you create a purpose, images and strategies will arise; this is how the mind works to attain something. Care should be taken, however, that they remain flexible and consistent with your purpose rather than letting your purpose become simply the accomplishment of these images and goals.

For example, perhaps I create the purpose for my intimate relationship to be mentally and emotionally connected to my partner and for us to experience being in union with one another. We can see that images might well pop up and how easily this purpose could lead to fantasies. I might imagine an always loving and supportive relating, perhaps with sunshine and flowers, overflowing with positive good feelings or some such. Yet none of that has to happen and may well be unrealistic. All that has to occur is to connect with my partner, no matter how it looks or what it feels like. See the difference? If I get stuck with an image that arises, I may well be disappointed in the outcome and miss the fact that the image has nothing to do with my purpose.

Our agenda drives are often quite strong and tend to override any created purpose, especially because creating a purpose often starts out intellectually and this doesn't have the power that our emotional drives have. So how can we create a purpose without our agenda running the show?

If we develop the ability to experience another, a circumstance, or objects for themselves we free our perception from automatically relating what's there to ourselves. From this perspective, we can more readily create a purpose free of our agenda's influence. Using this untethered experience, we can ask: What is wanted and needed? What would I like to commit my life to? What purpose can I create for this relationship, As we dwell on such questions we may come up with observations or ideas that are new and unexpected.

Even when such a revelation is not forthcoming, if you learn to feel your reactions as your own and not as caused by circumstance or others, then you are freer to create your relationship to life. You might also start considering the creation of a purpose by asking other questions such as: Why enter into this domain in the first place? What kind of experience do I want to nurture in such and such? What is it that I want to achieve with a project or an endeavor, and why do I want to achieve that? What is it that can be created that hasn't been created yet, and how can it be created without my self getting in the way? These kinds of questions help ballpark a direction for your consideration, and from there you might more clearly see what purpose would be consistent with achieving such an experience.

Once you create and clarify your purpose for anything, you can then be appropriate by behaving and taking action consistent with that purpose. The purpose for any activity determines if an action is appropriate or not. But how do you know what is appropriate in each case? Actions must relate to what's there in a way that realizes your goals and stays true to your purpose. If you are not currently interacting so that you are on purpose—actively working toward realizing your current objectives—then your actions are inappropriate.

As we will see in the next section, "Staying on Point," being on purpose means you stay consistent with your aims instead of getting off track or distracted and pursuing action that has nothing to do with what you are trying to accomplish. When you stray off purpose you need to notice that as soon as possible and get back on track.

To be sure, staying on purpose doesn't mean failure is not an option. As we will see with the principle of "Correction," something is seen as a failure when it is not accomplishing whatever goal is at hand. Yet even if the attempt fails to accomplish what you intended, it might still be on purpose as an attempt to realize the goal. From this attempt you get feedback, adjust your method, and try again. By learning and correcting your course of action, you stay on purpose.

Consider what you might create as a purpose in various domains of your experience, like your purpose for an intimate partnership, or for your career or work, perhaps even a purpose for recreating. What would you create? For example, perhaps a purpose for your primary intimate relationship could be, "to share my life in partnership with another as we learn to grow together, and I learn to transcend my exclusive self-focus in the process." A possible purpose for work could be, "to provide growth opportunities and increased consciousness for others, while I continue to learn and grow in the process." In recreation although your purpose may be to have fun, it could also be, "to engage in enlivening activities that push me to expand my sense of self while enjoying the company of others."

Creating a Purpose Exercise

Come up with a purpose for whatever activities are central to your life—relationships, projects, hobbies, career, whatever. Once you have a clear formulation of a purpose, contemplate what actions, thinking, and feelings you've been engaging within that domain that are inappropriate for realizing or being consistent with your purpose. If you are serious about what you want to be up to, then those activities will need to change, won't they? Now, consider what might be appropriate thoughts, feelings, and actions instead.

Having played it out in your mind you should have a better sense of what kinds of activities—both mental and physical—would be consistent with your purpose. Remember not to get stuck on an image or fantasy. If you come up with a sentence or description of a purpose, over time as things unfold you may see a need to reword it. Remember the purpose you intend is what you want to create and be up to, your ability to describe it is secondary. It is useful to get clear in language to pin yourself down and also create clarity in what your purpose really is. Otherwise, it is likely to remain vague and subject to impulses based upon an agenda, not a purpose. But the sentence or statement shouldn't be confused with the purpose, it is only trying to represent it and give it specific form.

We frequently underestimate the power of purpose. We also often overlook the power of being clear about our ability to create one and stay with it. Purpose gives us clarity in life so that our thinking and actions can be directed appropriately and enables us to discover when they are not. When we allow the mind to run amok and are driven by unconscious agendas, even the things we cherish most—such as our close relationships and the passions we pursue—can get badly gummed up and produce results that only cause suffering, without us realizing where or how we got off track. Being able to see this principle in action—making a distinction between the effectiveness of being on purpose and the ineffectual agenda-driven world or the lazy and hapless world of "winging" it—we are able to correct this setback.

STAYING ON POINT

One power we can have in any conversation, investigation, or contemplation is to stay with a particular subject. There are many ways we get distracted or stray off the subject, especially if the subject is difficult or slippery. This can go unnoticed and if we don't notice we have slipped off topic it is difficult to stay on point.

Staying on point means whatever subject you are addressing remains central to your consideration or your speaking if you're having a conversation. The simplest version of this is to keep your speaking or investigation on topic. If you know what the topic is then stay with that subject until it's resolved. If you are trying to solve a problem with someone, for example, then keep addressing the problem and stay wed to solving it until you are done.

This same dynamic applies to all kinds of interactions or investigations. Although many people find it challenging to keep their focus on a particular subject without wandering off, staying on point often involves more skill and attentiveness than just staying with a subject. Within interactions, learning to ask the right questions and being attentive to the nature of the responses is a skill we need in order to navigate successfully to a desired goal.

Let's look at how this might play out using a simple example of asking where the bathroom is. In such a conversation it is unlikely we would get off course, but if at the end of the dialogue you still don't know where the bathroom is, then the speaking didn't do its job. If lots of descriptions are forwarded about the building or other information is offered but none of it clarifies where the bathroom is, then you were not on point. Sometimes this is due to distraction, or the conversation wanders to greener pastures without notice because something interesting replaces your mission. Sometimes there is a lack of clarity about whether or not the information offered is doing the job. Keeping a vigil on the subject, and simply asking yourself whether you now know where the bathroom is and can you get there, should reveal any digression.

You may have an image of or directions about where the bathroom is but if you still can't find it, this suggests that either the information was wrong or more than likely the images or conclusions and assumptions you made while receiving it were inaccurate, or both. A useful skill to develop is to be aware of this possible disconnect and to question the information-giver in such a way as to avoid this pitfall. If, in your mind, you can't clearly picture every step of physically moving from where you are to the place you want to go then there is something missing and you need to fill in the gaps. Also, ofttimes the provider of information makes assumptions and leaves out useful details because they know how to get there and it's easy for them to forget to include crucial aspects in their directions. As you listen, consider this may be happening and make sure you know all that you need to know to accomplish your task.

Once, quite some time ago, I was in Nicaragua during the Contra wars against the Sandinista; I was with the Sandinista. During my time there, I found the Nicaraguan people to be most gracious and generous with a high level of value placed on relationships. But they did not have many logistical skills, especially in warfare. I did. I have many stories of that time but the one that might apply here was about trying to get to a depot in the mountains. I was driving with my girlfriend, a Nicaraguan-American (which is why I was there in the first place, since her family and cousins were fighting with the Sandinistas), and we were lost.

We stopped to ask someone where the depot was. They generously gave us directions. But knowing accuracy wasn't their strong point, as we drove on, I insisted we ask another and another and another. After talking with four people, we were given directions that it was north, south, east, and west! I never felt their intent was to deceive but that the important thing was to help, to give something. Accuracy wasn't important, giving was. So obviously we needed at least a fifth opinion to break this impasse. When we stopped to ask an old man, his first words were "I'm not sure." I immediately said, "Wherever he tells us to go, we're going." His deliberate consideration and acknowledging the fact he could be wrong—which no one else did—made him a more reliable source. It turned out he was right. In any case, asking the right questions and listening well to the responses can make a difference in successfully getting to the desired outcome.

On a more humorous note, when I first moved to Texas, more than once as I asked for directions I ran into the same dysfunctional dynamic. I was told it was "down the road a piece," which I found was quite meaningless since it turned out "a piece" could mean less than a mile or a hundred miles. But the most fascinating thing was even after telling them that I was new to the area, they'd proceed to describe their directions in relation to what *used* to be there—like "you know where that old gas station used to be? Well, turn right just past there." Even when I said I had no idea where the gas station had been, they'd stick to that description. It was fascinating. Not helpful, but fascinating.

Of course, this principle applies to every interaction that addresses a particular subject—as opposed to wandering conversations in which the only goal is to connect with another and perhaps entertain each other—and not just getting directions. Being sensitive to and aware of what's being said, whether your questions are actually being responded to—and if not, revisiting them until they are—keeping a vigil on possible misunderstandings, and so on are necessary to stay on point as well as to avoid pitfalls and sidelines.

When it comes to contemplation the same basics apply. Confronting an apparently unyielding problem—when no matter how hard you try you cannot accomplish a task—the mind will move elsewhere, either searching for solutions or for distractions. This is a common occurrence in contemplation. The goal of contemplation is to instantly and directly become conscious of the nature of your subject. It is common, however, for this not to happen in the first moment, or the second, or sometimes a million moments. When this effort hits a wall of not knowing—not only not knowing the "answer" but also not knowing how to proceed or how to accomplish the task—the mind becomes frustrated because it has run out of options and doesn't know what to do. At this point any alternate direction becomes very tempting.

This is why the subject must be the only focus. Otherwise, the mind will keep switching subjects when it runs into such difficulties. Staying with the same subject no matter what comes up or how difficult it becomes, even when there seems no way to proceed, is important for contemplation, as well as any other pursuit where staying on point is a powerful tool for success.

INCREASING AWARENESS

I notice that most people seem to be far less aware of what's going on around them than they think. For example, in a store often it seems people focus on the task in front of them and don't perceive others or objects in motion around them. I have been known on more than one occasion to notice the lack of awareness in someone about to turn or move in a direction that will collide with another person or otherwise gum up the works, and so I'll casually reach out and tap their shoulder, thus ensuring their attention broadens. In this way, a crash or a challenging or embarrassing encounter is avoided. In such cases, I usually just slide on by and the other really doesn't know where the touch came from. But the problem is solved.

Awareness can apply across the board in our experience. There are many domains of awareness: being aware of the environment all around us, aware of the purpose of any activity or object, aware of the whole body and how our bodies work, aware of our own internal states and our patterns of behavior or reactions, and so on.

There are many benefits to increasing awareness. When we increase our awareness of any aspect of life, we are more accurate and inclusive in our assessments and so more effective in relating to what's there. We're not just aware of what's around us, but what the purpose is for any activity, what is wanted and needed, and so on. We are also more enabled to know what is happening in our bodies and more sensitive to subtle changes or influences. This body awareness has many benefits— increased balance, coordination, skill, more efficient movement, and so on. Being aware of our minds and emotions certainly allows us a much better way to cope with difficult stuff and better manage our experience.

Clearly, our degree of awareness in life makes our relationship to it effective or not, and yet when it comes to managing our daily living, we often get bogged down in so many subjective, conceptual, and social activities that our present awareness of anything objective is diminished. So it's useful to at least revisit from time to time this tendency to lose objective awareness and instead focus on increasing our awareness of the present—perhaps making this an ongoing practice—because we tend to slip unknowingly into being less aware of the present moment than we could be.

Long ago I had a friend who lived in the mountains off the grid. I would visit him for a few days at a time, and coming from the big city my mind would be racing as a matter of course. The pace in the mountains seemed excruciatingly slow. But over a few hours, I would calm down and in a day or two manage to simply sit on a log and watch a butterfly for quite some time. The shift seemed forced to begin with, but as my mind became focused to the physical and present reality before me, I really appreciated the shift and I'm sure it was good for me.

Awareness isn't consciousness. Through awareness alone we aren't conscious of the nature of anything nor are we more conscious of relative truths. But by being more aware, a door opens to greater consciousness should we seek it. When we contemplate, we almost always become much more aware and sensitive to our environment, bodies, and internal state because we are concentrating for longer than normal periods of time on the present moment and this produces an increase in awareness. As we steadily inquire and open up to "experience" whatever is true in this moment, there is nowhere for our attention to go but onto whatever we are aware of. As we probe into this moment, attempting greater consciousness, a side effect of this effort is an increased awareness and sensitivity. The awareness itself doesn't necessarily produce consciousness but it certainly doesn't hurt and always boosts our sensitivity to our present experience and our contemplative efforts.

CREATIVITY AND CHANGE

One thing I think most people don't grasp is the possibility that they can actually create their experience in many ways—simply doing the work in ending suffering dramatically changes your experience at least.

Some aspects of experience can be created from nothing. Others that you don't seem able to create from scratch can still be influenced significantly. When dealing with your perceptive faculties, which are founded on biological organs interacting with the laws of physics, you will be subject to these realities and so your perceptions will conform to biological parameters. You will get what you get and you can't really change that.

Certainly, you could have disabilities or broken organs that either make it impossible or difficult for you to match the facilities of those without these maladies. You might also have a more refined or sensitive faculty than most, and maybe even a faculty that others generally don't have, but these are rare and even when occurring you are still stuck with the parameters and framework of those specific capacities.

It is also possible for you to increase your perceptive sensitivity and to increase your awareness. Increasing these abilities is a function of practice and attention. Yet when I speak of creating experience, such improvements in your abilities are not primarily what I'm talking about. Even about those aspects of perception that you don't seem to be able to change, your relationship to and interpretation of what's perceived is not fixed. How you hold and relate to what you perceive is changeable.

What you think, assume, believe, or feel, and your perspective, your moods, and the like, are all possible to change, influence, eliminate, or create. These activities constitute most of what seems like your objective experience and all of your subjective experience. So when it comes to creating or changing your experience in some way, there is much you can do.

For example, people often think that if they are bored, upset, depressed, or whatever, then that is simply what they get because it is what they have. I remember telling one of my apprentices to be enthusiastic when he wasn't. He thought I was nuts. How can someone be enthusiastic when they aren't enthusiastic? As the months rolled by and with more work, he finally got that he could simply create being enthusiastic. This was a significant breakthrough for him. Instead of holding one's mood or disposition as circumstantially derived, grasping that it is something you are generating allows you to alter what you generate.

Since your state of mind and emotions are relating to circumstance, they will generally unfold as is indicated by your self-survival and self-agenda. That's their purpose. Left alone, this is what will happen. Certainly, if you change something about your agenda—your needs or concerns, your outlook on life, your self-esteem, and so on—then your mental-emotional responses to various circumstances will also change to some degree.

Barring that, however, reactions will continue and states will arise consistent with familiar patterns. It is good to practice changing any reaction or state that you have, not just to change that particular state but to know that such change is possible in all cases. This way you will relate to every state differently even when you don't change them.

Earlier I talked about "mastering" emotions, learning to spontaneously switch from emotion to emotion to emotion. This is learning to be creative within your experience rather than merely reactive. Just so, other aspects of your experience can also be changed simply by an act of will.

Yet, to be clear, although being able to change your experience is very useful, it is also useful to understand why such changes don't readily occur. You may be sick of hearing me refer to self-survival, even though its own name is the very reason it sounds so dramatic and death-defying. Perhaps another word such as "life" might be more openly received because it is the same principle as self-survival but life is something usually desired and embraced. This principle applies to even the mundane and minor stuff that composes our experience. Regardless of the word used, the reality of this fundamental force must be grasped in order to understand why your experience so consistently goes down the same mental-emotional roads.

I know this is hard to grasp deeply, but it is what keeps all of us pressed into circumstantially derived characteristic experiences. Without the dynamic of persisting as yourself—managing life by relating everything to what you experience as yourself—change is far more easily accessible. Remember, this "self" that determines your experience includes all the beliefs and assumptions you have about you and world. Letting go of at least some of this makes creating something else more likely.

Sometimes it might be difficult to change your direction when you feel stuck in some groove or flow of experience that may not be the healthiest or most effective form to take. It may require some time to focus and come to grips with the fact that—even though it feels as if such reactions or moods or perspectives are necessary or justified by circumstance—they are actually only that way because of self-interest and self-concerns. Once you really get this, it becomes easier to make a change in your experience.

Whether it takes time—a few minutes or longer—or can be done instantly, the result is the same. Your experience is changed. Of course, this is generally shifting from one known experience to another known experience, like changing from anger to love, or moving from a biased and closed view to a nonjudgmental and open perspective, or from one idea or belief to another or to a state of not-knowing. This is an extremely powerful skill for living life. Yet beyond managing your internal experience (and so expressions and behavior), it is also possible to create something not yet created. But that is the subject for another time.

CHAPTER NINE

Powerful Life-Enhancing Principles

THERE ARE MANY POWERFUL PRINCIPLES that can dramatically change and enhance one's experience of life. In order for them to work, however, they have to be adopted and lived as part of your character or person. For that to happen you have to understand what the principle is and be willing to commit yourself to adopting it. This can't be done without seeing the value and power available in doing so. Like the above distinctions, the following principles will be a lot to take on. It is very unlikely you will be able to incorporate them all into your person. You can try them all on and get to know them experientially, grasping their value and power and so altering your perspective on matters related to them. But more likely you'll be best served, at least in the beginning, by focusing on one or two principles to adopt and incorporate as an aspect of the life you live. So what is a principle and how can it be applied to life?

Before considering principles to adopt, we should better understand what a principle is. This section was originally written for my book *The Art of Mastery*, but since we are going to look at several principles here, I borrowed it and edited it a bit to fit with our work here. I think it will contribute to your success in understanding and adopting a principle.

PRACTICE, PRINCIPLE, BEING

When it comes to trying to consciously change your experience, there are three stages you should consider. Everyone knows that *practice*— repeatedly engaging in actions attempting to be effective in some way—is essential to the process of becoming skillful at something. The statement "practice makes perfect" embodies this sentiment. What most people overlook, however, is that it isn't just practice alone that gets the job done. When someone accomplishes some change in their experience they have probably consciously, or unconsciously, made two more shifts.

Practice implies lots of repetition, doing something again and again attempting to accomplish a result—often falling short, making correction, and trying again. Over time you begin to improve but an even more significant shift starts to emerge. After some success with various circumstances, you may become privy to the principle(s) behind how this activity works.

Consciously searching for and contemplating the principles that produce certain outcomes greatly increases your likelihood of finding them. Once you experience a principle you can then begin to act from that principle. When an effective principle governs your actions, success is almost inevitable.

Before going into specific principles, perhaps it would be useful to consider what I'm referring to *as* a principle. Let's start by looking at traditional definitions of principle that may apply.

Principle

ORIGIN from Latin *principium*, "source,"
principia (plural), "foundations"

- a fundamental truth that serves as the foundation for a system of behavior or for a chain of reasoning
- a rule governing one's personal behavior

- a general scientific theorem or law that has numerous special applications across a wide field
- a natural law forming the basis for the construction or working of a machine
- a fundamental source or basis of something
- a fundamental quality or attribute determining the nature of something; an essence

From the definitions, you should begin to glean the arena that is a principle. Here, a principle is what dominates your experience and actions so that these unfold in a particular way. The principle demands that your actions are consistent with it in order for it to manifest. Because the principle needs to dominate your actions in order for you to be effective, it must also dominate your experience—since your perceptive-experience is what determines your actions. In order to do that, you have to experience what the principle really is as itself—and adopt it.

In this way, your state of mind becomes consistent with the principle because your perceptions must recognize the distinctions that allow you to follow that principle. You'll perceive what's occurring in relation to the principle and take actions in response consistent with it—that is the purpose for adopting a principle. A principle is what has interaction turn out some way without fail. To illustrate, I will use two examples of principles: gravity and honor. One is a law of physics, the other a social possibility.

You can see that as long as you're on this, or any other, planet you have no choice but to relate to the principle of gravity if you want to manage such acts as standing and walking. In our world, this principle is a given, and everyone must align to it in some way. Such a principle is not adopted but adapted to. To master an activity where gravity is a core element, however, you must refine and improve your relationship to it, and your every action needs to be dominated by that principle.

In the case of honor, this is a principle you have to adopt or create—rather than simply align to it as you must with gravity—and the only way it works is if you surrender to the demands of honor. You have honor only when it shows up in your experience and behavior and dictates what you do and don't do. The principle doesn't exist anywhere else, only in what you do; yet the principle isn't the act itself, it is what dictates the act.

Adopting a principle means your experience can no longer be subject to the usual seemingly random and self-oriented whims and impulses that are familiar, arising from the private world of your inner self. This common self-experience is often thought to be the only possibility available for people—save for applying discipline and willpower to temporarily override it.

Yet consider a new possibility, such as adopting a principle that is as steadfast as gravity dominating your entire experience. You can see that with gravity things always fall down and every object is aligned with this force. This is not an option. As long as the principle is active, all experience and action will be aligned with it and dominated by it. It has to be the same for any adopted principles if they are going to be effective.

You can't be effective with any principle unless you experience it for what it is. This means separating out any baggage the word or concept might bring along. If you only intellectually or conceptually understand the principle, you will fail to make it work. To be effective, a principle cannot be about morality or beliefs. It can't be grasped if you add personal reactions.

A principle doesn't care about you, nor is it necessarily designed to benefit you or your agenda. The principle may well not be consistent with your belief systems, and you should not try to fit it into your views about the way the world should work. When everything that is not the principle itself—only and simply—is stripped away you are left with the principle. A principle is a principle. It is not good or bad, it is simply that.

Of course, you adopt a principle to serve you, but it won't serve you and has no real power if it isn't allowed to be what it is. It won't work if you don't experience and surrender to it *as* itself. This means you must let go of anything inconsistent with the principle even if you desire for it to be otherwise. It is important that you *experience* the principle, not just understand it, and that your disposition, state, and actions are dominated by and consistent with it. When you do that, your experience will be different, you will recognize the principle acting in relation to circumstance, and you will immediately have different results.

Let's look more deeply into the two aforementioned examples of principles to see how they would show up in your experience. Starting with the principle of gravity, you can see that your every physical action on this planet revolves around aligning with gravity. Since you were born this has been the case, and although you may not remember, you practiced again and again to align with and master this principle. Eventually you became successful at performing the actions you were attempting—standing, walking, and so on. But because all of this was done without any real consciousness of the principle, except for the demands it placed on you, you may have stopped progressing to a more refined degree once you mastered the basics.

If you were to take up tightrope walking, for example, you find more practice and probably more conscious sensitivity to this principle is necessary to accomplish that art and certainly to attain mastery in it. When you consciously search out an experience of the principle, you can improve, and even master, your relationship to gravity so that your physical actions are perfectly aligned with the principle and you can perform feats related to gravity that most people can't. As an aside, after I won the full-contact World Championships and returned to my girlfriend of the time—a Pan Am flight attendant and TV producer—at some point I showed her movies of the event. Her comment was, "I don't know anything about martial arts; what I see is a man with incredible balance."

Yet there are many principles that don't require alignment due to physics—such as socially created principles or invented principles that apply to both physical and nonphysical arenas. There may also be principles operating presently in your life activities that you don't know about. Mastering your experience demands that this condition of ignorance change.

There are many possible principles that create powerful abilities in various domains—physical, social, business, mental, emotional, and more. Many of the principles that work in the physical domain also work, in a different form, in mental, social, or business domains. A sampling of a few principles that make a significant difference in many domains are honesty, integrity, letting go, listening, being calm, inclusion, acceptance, joining, and so on.

To better ground how elective principles work, let's take a deeper look into the socially created principle I brought up earlier and see how it might affect your experience if adopted. Honor is a principle that may seem antiquated and receding as an active or common principle in our modern culture. When we hear a word such as "honor," we immediately have ideas about what it means that are likely to include associations with morality and traditions. Yet if we are to experience the principle itself, we need to strip away all such associations or any other baggage that may be attached.

A principle doesn't have to "look" a certain way. When some socalled principle has to take a particular form then that would be a "tradition" or cultural custom or personal routine. These are not principles but dogmas or rituals. The principle, on the other hand, may or may not be operating within these rituals. A principle is what governs activity to unfold in a way consistent with the demands of that principle.

With honor, what is the principle? For someone to have honor it seems they must adhere to parameters of behavior that are confined to and demanded by this principle. Being honorable means being consistent with honest representation and principled interactions—doing the right thing, keeping your word, and conducting yourself in an honest and transparent manner. This means one's self is not the defining factor, but something bigger than the impulses, desires, and needs of the self. Lying is unacceptable, deceit beneath you, doing anything to hurt someone behind their back is disgraceful. These things are just not done, even if doing so would benefit you and not doing so may bring you harm or discomfort. This principle creates a much larger sense of self because it is not restricted to individual needs and agendas but to a far more inclusive, open, and transparent sense of being. Are you beginning to glean the principle I'm talking about?

You need to take care not to conflate traditional affectations or stances with being honorable. They may or may not be. What makes them honorable is the principle governing your behavior, not posturing or showy expressions. Honesty, doing the right thing (which is inclusive, serving everyone involved not just an individual), fair play, being bound to one's word no matter what, being transparent and straightforward without using indirect manipulations couched in acceptable sounding verbiage serving a deceitful agenda not immediately apparent—these are all behaviors consistent with the principle of honor. Can you see the dramatic influence on your experience this would have?

You might think that this principle would only affect your behavior, but this is far from true. Living and acting within the principle of honor requires that your thinking and emotions are also consistent with it. For example, an attitude of deceit would be seen as repugnant to you and so would be internally rejected. The thought to consider dishonorable behavior would be toxic and therefore either wouldn't arise, or if it did, would elicit feelings of guilt or shame and also be rejected, and so on. You can see that your thoughts and feelings would definitely be influenced by the principle.

What's more, self-esteem would rise dramatically, integrity would be an active aspect of your self-experience and so your internal state would tend to be consistent with your expressions because you are not engaging in exclusive self-serving or deceitful expressions or impulses. So the principle would definitely affect your internal state and self-experience as well as your behavior.

That is an example of one principle you can see would greatly influence your social experience and make a huge difference in your self and life experiences. That's how principles work. Imagine what would occur if you adopted any of a number of principles, such as those mentioned earlier and others specific to and effective in your pursuits and life.

In any case, now that you have an idea of what a principle is and how an effective principle can change your experience and so actions, let's go back to the three stages. Again, the first stage is practice. With enough practice, and perhaps leaps of experiential insight, you begin to detect or create a principle or principles that determine the effectiveness of whatever you're practicing. Once you experience and can take a principle into action and validate its effectiveness, you are closing in on shifting to the next stage.

After you have practiced and contemplated enough to discover the principle, and further, practiced enough to experience and prove the principle to yourself, you can move into the stage of surrendering to it. Surrendering to the principle means you make the principle dominant over your internal state and actions. Once this is the case, you don't have to proceed in bits and pieces, deciding this or that and taking shots in the dark in your pursuits. The overall operational decisions are pretty much made since the principle decides and you simply choose the method of action to realize your objectives. Once you surrender to the principle you are now effective in any activity that relates to that principle. This is something you can do consciously and deliberately whenever appropriate.

Beyond this level of mastery, if you see a principle as a fundamental aspect you want to be central to your own self-experience and life, you can then adopt it as an aspect of yourself. In this way, you begin "living" the principle rather than simply adopting it to serve some particular endeavor. For example, perhaps you see that the principle of honesty is essential for an authentic experience of being alive and therefore decide to adopt and live within this principle as an aspect of your very person. At this point, there is no need to try to be honest; it is just a clear and obvious aspect of your experience. This is *living as* or *being* the principle.

Now that you understand what a principle is and the need to adopt it into your experience for it to work, apply that knowledge to the following—as well as our previous work on creating new distinctions.

EXCELLENCE AND MASTERY

Let's see if the pursuit of excellence or even mastery can be an effective or life-enhancing principle instead of an oppressive burden or ideal and how that might be so. We associate both mastery and excellence with doing something extremely well or producing an unusually high-quality result. It often has a moral quality and an elevated status associated with it. But what if we took away whatever may be culturally added to the simple fact of excellence and instead consider it in a more existential way? What are the consequences, results, and changes that occur when excellence is taken on as a principle that governs some area of your life?

No such principle needs to be adopted in order to live life. It only needs to be adopted to produce certain results. Here, if we use this principle to explore and pursue mastery in some specific area of life, or life in general, both mind and action must conform to a higher standard. The effects of this trend in mind and action tend to be both healing and enlivening. But why might that be the case?

First, we should consider what we mean by mastery and the accompanying element of excellence. Normally, mastery refers to the quality of being outstanding or extremely good, having a higher quality than normal. This is what connects it to excellence. We can see that when someone masters something or produces a masterpiece, we will consider it excellent. What is *that* quality? Is it accessible to all of us and not just the selective few that commit themselves and accomplish some form of mastery?

When we look at a masterpiece, we recognize quality that hits an unusually high bar and provides some aspect we see as excellent. What is it that the artist reaches for that produces this quality? Contemplating this kind of question might allow us access to this same perspective.

Of course, we don't have to master anything to engage excellence and shouldn't consider it rare or inaccessible. But we might want to consider the shift in perspective that must be adopted to pursue mastery, since it could contribute something valuable to our relationship with excellence. So what is it that we are really trying to accomplish by adopting a principle crafted around this distinction?

Obviously, we want a better experience of life and perhaps a more effective relationship to our personal world and pursuits. So how would excellence provide these? We see that such a principle draws an increase of attention to whatever we are interacting with. This tends to increase awareness. The drive toward excellence also tends to increase attention to detail and, as in mastery, pushes us to seek out the most efficient arrangement of those details, which leads to more effectiveness. For example, in my early days of trying to master martial arts I adopted a motto of accomplishing the results of a fight gracefully. I sensed that if I couldn't do it gracefully I was missing something important. It turned out this was an essential element needed for mastery.

Further, with excellence or mastery your actions are charged to live up to a higher standard as to what you produce and this connects you with quality, in your own mind and probably the minds of others. With this experience, you are likely to have much higher self-esteem and a better perspective on life. Of course, such commitment to excellence usually requires more effort and work than the alternative. But even if such effort requires more research and action, correction, and constant and meticulous improvement, this is balanced by the emotional uplift and increase in self-esteem that can provide energy for the endeavor— because in this way the world in which you live feeds you rather than depletes you.

Certainly, we don't want to become obsessed or wed to a strict form of excellence, developing something like OCD or an unreasonable need to make everything conform to some idea of "perfection"—which is an ideal not a principle, and those are totally different. This creates stress and usually makes interactions with others challenging and you unpopular. It also drains you rather than feeds you. There should be room for excellence to be found in forms that aren't precise and times when strict adherence to aspects such as neatness or organizing can be comfortably set aside.

As an analogy, my mother used to say that grace was having people feel comfortable around you no matter who they are or how different they are from you. Therefore, in this case, we see that grace is not wed to appearances or the form that it needs to take, but to the result. If we use that sentiment as a guide, we can see that when we make excellence into a weapon, or use it to make us feel superior, or as a way to control things, or use it to judge others, and so on, we have lost the essence and real function of excellence. Excellence loses a great deal of its benefits when it becomes pedantic or obsessive. It seems healthiest when we keep a balance between the pursuit of excellence and the acceptance that life often unfolds in chaotic fashion.

It might also work best to have some vital areas of life adhere to excellence or the pursuit of mastery and allow others that aren't so important to you to be more "organic." Still, we shouldn't overlook the mental and emotional drain that being slovenly, lazy, or sloppy produce. Although it seems these traits are naturally "relaxed," the outcome and stress it puts on life and effectiveness and your relations with others—usually extending to not keeping your word and not committing to anything—creates often overlooked suffering. It seems a healthy balance needs to be had between the pursuit of excellence and the organic nature of life. Such a principle, whether it is the pursuit of excellence or the pursuit of mastery, pushes mind and action into learning far more than would otherwise occur.

RESPONSIBILITY

Responsibility is a well-known principle for governing our behavior and attitude. As a common notion, however, it is sometimes resisted or misunderstood. It often comes across as a burden or blame. If we strip away such misinterpretations, we can see responsibility in a different light.

Responsibility as a principle simply means you are held as the source of your own actions or your relationship to things. This is not a moral issue; it is simply acknowledging the facts and moving yourself into alignment with the principle. In so doing, you tend not to resist, deny, or try to get around this fact, but instead use it by involving yourself in consciously taking charge of your actions and internal states.

Once adhering to the principle of being responsible for your perspective, actions, reactions, assumptions, thought processes, and so on, you are in the strongest position to make changes, be more effective, or manage consequences. A side effect of adopting such a principle is an increase in self-esteem and a sense of being more powerful and in charge of your own life, even if sometimes you suffer unpleasant or embarrassing outcomes. This is because as the source of your experience and actions—which includes being responsible for influencing a great deal of what happens around you—you are in the driver's seat.

Of course, it means negative outcomes that you produce are also your responsibility. But as the "driver" you are empowered to steer the outcomes toward something more positive, or at least acknowledge the outcomes you've fostered and take responsibility for them. By owning them they are accepted for what they are. In this way, you can make correction and move on more smoothly than if you try to duck or resist your responsibility in the matter. Consider responsibility as a power you can take on, rather than an accusation leveled at you. Can you see the huge difference between these two dispositions?

INTENTION AND COMMITMENT

We have visited both intention and commitment, realizing them as important principles to help us turn conceptual-activity, which creates suffering, into conceptual-action, which doesn't. These are powerful distinctions to make and adopt for many aspects of life, so let's spend some time going into them a bit more deeply.

Intention often seems to be misunderstood. People generally think intention is simply the desire or thought to do something, or has to be emotionally motivated, or perhaps is a function of a strong will. Although emotion and willfulness may arise when you intend to create or do something, they actually aren't necessary, and intention isn't just a desire or thought. Intention is something you create, simply and without fanfare. Once the conceptual formation has occurred that contains the subject of intent, the only action necessary is to realize it. The impulse to take action is intention.

For example, if you want to lift your hand, the idea to do so must arise—but don't confuse this domain of conceptualization with "having a thought," or creating an image, or a memory, or an internal sentence, or any other conceptual process, which are all unnecessary. This idea can arise subconsciously and go almost unnoticed and very often does. It is pretty much the same act as the intention itself, the only addition the idea provides is the intended subject—which in this case is lifting the hand. When the idea forms into an intent it creates the impulse to do something. As you can see when you lift your hand, the intent is almost indistinguishable from the action because it arises virtually at the same time. Check it out.

As you do, make a distinction between a thought you might have to lift your hand and the actual intent to lift it. The thought itself is an abstraction and doesn't get the job done. When you lift the hand, then you have created intention. The intent is what generates the impulse or action, and so when the intent occurs so does the action. Although intention may be a fact of life, your disposition to it makes a huge difference in how you relate to it.

One mistake we make is to think that intent arises as a desire to do something whether it is done or not. A desire is not intent, it is a desire. Wanting to do something is not the same thing as intending to do it. Only setting out to actually do it indicates intention. This way of holding intent creates a distinction between desiring and doing. If nothing else, this distinction supports being responsible for one's actions without the excuse of, "well, I intended to, but . . ." No matter what the excuse is, it is still just an excuse, not an action. What makes things happen is action, not excuses, and intent creates the impulse that produces action.

Try not to see this view of intent as a moral or even strategic decision but as a fact. Study when you take some form of action—physical, emotional, or conceptual—and notice the intent to make it happen. This is intent. When some action doesn't take place, notice there is no intent, even if there is the idea to do it or a desire to do it. Of course, there may be an intent to act that early on gets short-circuited for some reason and only the beginnings of the act occur, but then notice the intent also stops or has been redirected to a different purpose. Seeing intent in this way takes the ambiguity out of it. It's also important to get that intent is something created and can be consciously created to serve a purpose that otherwise might remain dormant due to lack of action.

Commitment, on the other hand, is needed to produce results, usually more long-term results than a simple action can accomplish. Action only produces the result of the action itself. A conceived goal that requires more than one simple act demands a commitment to creative processes involving all of the actions needed to produce that desired result.

Intent and commitment aren't the same thing but do work together. Intent creates specific action, and commitment produces a particular result. Obviously, action, through intent, is necessary for any commitment to take place. Commitment on the other hand is dedicating a part of your life—energy, time, and activity—to producing a particular result. Commitment is a principle that has to be adopted.

One way to look at the difference can be seen at a picnic. Sitting at a picnic table, you might intend to grab a Styrofoam cup that is there and reach out to do so. If you grab the cup then it is a done deal and the result of grabbing it realizes the intent. On the other hand, a wind could blow the cup away as you reach for it. You intended to grab the cup as it was, but circumstances have changed and perhaps you decide to let the cup go and intend to scratch your nose instead. If you were committed to grabbing the cup, however, you'd chase it down until you got it no matter the changes in circumstance.

A commitment may take a considerable amount of time and action, or very little. It may involve many changes and corrections to make it happen, or it could take a simple process to accomplish the result. Commitment is giving your life energies to bringing something into existence through action and creativity. Committing to a goal demands you devote whatever is needed of your time and energy to having it come about.

For example, I might commit myself to mastering an art. We can see that such a commitment won't be realized with one moment of intent and action. Certainly, I must intend to take action toward that end, but I will likely have to take many, many actions—not only physical action, but also mental action to create learning, understanding, new perspectives, states, lots of correction, and so on—to pursue my goal of mastery. Without commitment that isn't possible.

This doesn't mean that problems and obstacles won't arise. They may well, and some might arise because of the commitment. If you aren't committed, your path forward is open-ended and if something gets in your way you can just do something else. But when you are on a committed path you are required to persist even if something blocks your way forward or difficulties arise. When you are committed to a course of action, obstacles aren't a problem, they are something to resolve. Your mind might also have resistance to something asked of you by the commitment and you may freak out or be upset in some fashion because of it. Commitment, however, gets you through the obstacles and past the breakdowns. That's what commitment is about.

Clarifying the nature and reality of intention and consciously activating the principle of commitment gives you powerful tools for creating life rather than just suffering it. It tends to eliminate the excuses and procrastination that keep you from clear and effective action. It also assists you in not getting bogged down in ineffective actions that don't accomplish the goals you set. When repeated feedback suggests that your actions are not on purpose—meaning they are not consistent with producing the desired result—then commitment demands learning and correction, changing your actions until you effectively accomplish your goal.

Sometimes people say they want to commit or to do something but just can't or don't seem to be able to get around to it. If you find you're saying to yourself you want to do something but aren't doing it, then stop saying that! You don't want to do it if you aren't going to do it. When you really intend to do it, you will do it. Until then there is no need to beat yourself up with notions of wanting but not doing.

We might say commensurate with commitment is discipline. Discipline really arises naturally when you are committed. Discipline is doing anything that wouldn't just befall you. What drives you to do this or that—following your whims or reacting to circumstances and so on—are all actions that befall you, meaning they happen naturally and automatically without any real consideration or decision on your part. You see it as just living life, with your experience determined by whatever happens to arise circumstantially. To do anything other than that requires discipline.

Sometimes we hear "discipline" as harsh, demanding, or perhaps as punishment. Try not to hear it that way. Consider that simply pursuing something by committing yourself to pursuing it is a discipline. Perhaps the added element discipline brings to the table is generating the idea that a certain method, path, routine, effort, or a particular endeavor will lead to the results to which you are committed. In that case, discipline is committing yourself to that path. But be open to the possibility that you may not be correct about the path you choose and that you might have to change your method. But, of course, you have to give your adopted method a genuine try until you have experienced the reality behind it—discovering whether it is functional or not.

For example, say you want to master a martial art, so you commit to doing so. You determine that attending classes at a school with a master will move you in that direction. So commensurate with your commitment, you take on the discipline of going to class and training every day without fail. If you only did what you felt like doing you would probably miss many classes because you wouldn't always feel like going. This is the difference between discipline and what befalls you.

In your studies, however, you may discover that the art you are studying isn't full enough and so isn't going to get you where you want to go. Then, consistent with your commitment, you find one that will or invent whatever is necessary to make it happen. This is your commitment acting to change the discipline as is appropriate to pursue your goals. Discipline is really just an extension of commitment, serving the purpose of taking on a regimen of committed action toward some end.

HONESTY, HONOR, INTEGRITY

Of course, each of these is its own principle, and I have addressed them all in other places. So here I want to emphasize the power of such principles to transform your life as well as the world around you. As suggested, such principles shouldn't be adopted to try to be a good or moral person, but to create a far more effective and powerful life, and not only for you but for all those you associate with as well. Remember, you influence those around you with your behavior and actions, and these are based on the standards and principles that guide your choices.

When honesty becomes an actual principle for your thinking and speaking, rather than simply an action you do or don't do, it dramatically alters your experience, communications, and interactions. Why would I say "alter"? I suspect that more than one person will react by thinking they are already honest and so nothing would change. Yet, as far as I can tell, very few "honest" people are truly as honest as they think. Real honesty is more of a practice than an aspect of personal identity. It is about itself, not about serving the person or making one look "good."

The principle honors only what's true, not a self. Conflict is likely to occur between what's true and self-agenda needs or fears. Adopting and committing to this principle requires adherence to whatever is true even when it doesn't serve the self. Of course, there are many ways to use or manipulate facts that can make truth-telling a weapon and not a communication of the truth, so care has to be taken not to fall into the trap of using "telling the truth" as a weapon or manipulation. When that's done, it's not the truth, nor is it honest. This is akin to using the letter of the law to do harm rather than to realize and be true to the intent or purpose of that same law.

Unfortunately, social machinations as well as social conventions may require communications that aren't black-and-white recitations of the facts but something more nuanced. It may be that what is most empowering, as well as having more fidelity to the truth, demands a socially complex expression, rather like poetry as opposed to prose. Of course, this distinction itself leaves room open to mislead or misrepresent, but that is just more of the same dynamic of manipulating (and so, lying) while pretending to use the truth to do it.

So the line of when to express the truth and how to express it is a decision everyone must make themselves depending on circumstance. But this "choice" often ends up being used as self-protection rather than an adherence to the principle. The starting point should be a blunt thinking and speaking whatever is true as it is, unaltered. This can quite naturally be tempered with what is socially acceptable or to spare someone unnecessary discomfort—the operative word being "unnecessary," meaning the truth is not diminished or compromised, simply kept to oneself or couched in softer terms than one might otherwise use if another's feelings or esteem were not involved. In some rare cases, the presentation of what's true might have to be carefully crafted in order for justice to be served.

Social concerns aside, honesty requires a straightforward commitment to speaking and even thinking in alignment with what's true. The most important focus must always be on being honest with oneself and to oneself—far more than when speaking to others. Brutal self-honesty is necessary long before opening one's mouth. When you are honest with yourself, many thoughts, desires, needs, actions, and speaking that normally just serve a self without regard for the truth may have to be altered or tossed. As well, fears, embarrassing things, uncomfortable encounters or revelations may need to be embraced. Imagine the overwhelming dominating influence such an operating principle would have for you and your experience of life.

The most central element of honesty is often overlooked—namely, honesty relates to what's true. We can see when we mix in morality and social status and such, we can miss this connection in favor of the "act" of being honest. Yet if we don't adhere to what's true as best we can, we are not being honest. Truth is about "what is." This moves honesty from a social activity to an existential one. Consider this.

Sometimes people want to dedicate themselves to such deep honesty but run into the problem of thinking they need to reveal everything that comes to mind. No one wants to hear everything that comes to mind, not even the one to which it comes. Simply puking out every thought or feeling that comes up when it comes up really should be saved for a therapist.

As said, being honest with yourself is the most important aspect, and when you study yourself you might find that sometimes it can be difficult to know what is true. Therefore, there is no need to share that with others until you are clear yourself and are also clear about your purpose for sharing it. After I had a deep breakthrough (called enlightenment in certain circles) of the nature of existence or reality, at some point I began to notice I couldn't actually speak the truth. So I didn't speak for about two weeks, struggling with this issue. Eventually I simply worked to do the best I could and represent myself honestly, even if I couldn't match an absolute truth in my speaking. As I have said, honesty is more of a practice, something you can get better and better at, than it is a stance to take. You have to sort all these things out for yourself.

Just so, the principles of honor and integrity have the same effect. I touched on honor earlier, and integrity relates directly to honesty and keeping one's word. The point is, these principles influence your experience of self and life, especially within the social domain. Although it may be difficult to imagine such a change, if you truly grasp what the principle is, you can adopt it and get a firsthand experience—or at least imagine doing so. Yet through imagination it might be harder to grasp how this adoption would be more effective and powerful than what may currently determine your behavior.

Why are these principles effective and powerful? Working with principles that demand an adherence to what's really so, and precisely so, as well as principles that make one's intent and actions transparent and trustworthy, all create a more accurate assessment of unfolding circumstances and more trust within your interactions. This leads to being more effective and authentic in the real world.

Remember, the principle serves itself not you. When you adopt such a principle it is clear you are adhering to something independent from your personal needs and concerns, you aren't just self-serving. This transforms your experience of yourself as well as how others see you. Your experience and self-esteem become far more seamless and powerful. Without having so many things to protect, lies to hide, spin to promote, weaknesses to cover up, and so on, your transparency and wholeness—and so experience and character—becomes unassailable, and this increases the sense and the reality of your personal power. But again, that is all a side effect. It is the principle that is the source of this transformation.

> *Be Impeccable with your Word. Speak with integrity.*
> *Say only what you mean. Avoid using the word to speak*
> *against yourself or to gossip about others. Use the power of*
> *your word in the direction of truth and love.*
>
> DON MIGUEL RUIZ

CORRECTION

Pursuing any domain of learning requires correction. Unlike *Apollo 13*, failure *is* an option—not only an option but an essential part of any successful pursuit to learn or discover anything. What makes failure useful, rather than just putting an end to the attempt to be successful, is correction.

For example, whenever we pursue some attainment, such as mastering an activity, there is very little chance that our first attempts will achieve any level of mastery. The attempt is essential, however, for without it nothing moves forward or becomes real. What moves it from an ineffective attempt toward mastery is most often a new attempt that is different in some way from the first, either as an experiment to get more feedback or a corrected course that promises more success.

Progress most often occurs in relationship to failures—from which we learn and make correction, altering our actions to keep moving forward. It might be nice if we could be completely successful or masterful in our first attempt, but since that isn't likely, we depend on correction to make progress. Correction is a principle necessary for learning as well as for attaining any degree of mastery. Without resisting failure—even as we attempt to avoid it—we waste no energy on unfruitful reactions or tantrums when it occurs. Instead, we are eager to acknowledge failures and embrace correction because we recognize this is our way to success. (For a more in-depth look into correction, see my book *The Art of Mastery*.)

EMPOWERMENT

An interactive or social principle we can create is to empower others. To empower someone in this context is to relate, communicate, and facilitate another person to become conscious of something for themselves, or assist them in becoming more effective or creative. Generally, it involves communicating for the purpose of enhancing another's experience of their own consciousness, personal power, or creativity.

If I'm communicating with you, then the experience I have will be shared with you, and if you actually receive this communication, then you will grasp it and experience it for yourself. Therefore, if I experience in you a possibility for transformation or increased consciousness and I help draw your attention to what's there, you will have that same experience for yourself. Stated more simply, if I recognize in you a possibility or potential and show that to you, you will experience this possibility or potential for yourself. This is empowering another.

We may not often actually want to do something just for the benefit of another. Of course, we do get to feel good about ourselves and usually get positive feedback and gratitude from the other if it works out and they acknowledge our contribution. Yet another, more "selfish" reason for doing so is that over time we begin to be surrounded by and to relate to more effective, powerful, and conscious people, and this empowers our environment. The more effective and conscious those around us are, the more we as a community can get done and so the more effective we can be.

Of course, we should make a distinction between empowering someone and simply flattering or encouraging them. On occasion, it may be appropriate to encourage and motivate someone to give them a boost in their efforts at some task. It might even be appropriate to flatter someone to increase their self-esteem in order to help them through some difficult time. When such actions are taken, however, I think it is important to find a way to stay as close to the truth as possible and be as realistic as you can in your communications and not just blow smoke up their chimney. Although these acts might be seen as minor types of empowerment, neither are what I'm talking about.

Instead, the principle of empowerment is based on the truth and what is real and really possible. It isn't making something up or hoping or fantasizing or projecting anything onto the other person. It is recognizing a reality in them or being conscious of something worth sharing that they themselves don't recognize and assisting them in recognizing and making it real for themselves.

PART V

❧

Practice

Almost all our suffering is the product of our thoughts. We spend nearly every moment of our lives lost in thought, and hostage to the character of those thoughts. You can break this spell, but it takes training just like it takes training to defend yourself against a physical assault.

SAM HARRIS

So far, we have looked into many subjects. But all of these considerations demand a deeper investigation than is common for most of us. This requires a lot of investigation, thought, and of course contemplation.

Without an ability to contemplate—to look past personal bias, thoughts, beliefs, and feelings to seek what is genuinely true—we are very unlikely to discover or understand all that has been asserted here. Therefore, we are called to take up a practice if we want to pursue understanding our reality to any depth. The kind of practice and how it's designed is open-ended—as long as its purpose is to directly grasp the truth—but there are principles that determine whether or not any practice can be successful.

CHAPTER TEN

Doing the Work

AS WE SAW IN THE SECTION ON PRINCIPLES, practice is key
to discovering and learning how to put a principle into action. We also
saw in exercises like "Mastering Emotions" (on page 141) the need for
practicing or training to improve our mind control. I'm sure it's clear
from our work on ending suffering that changing the concepts that generate suffering will take training and repetition for us to accomplish any
long-term transformation.

When it comes to mind or consciousness work, one place I think
people often get stuck is assuming that because they've heard or learned
about something it is enough. This is almost never the case. The mind
is patterned and much occurs automatically. Without repeatedly and
consciously training a new way of thinking or a new perspective, we
aren't likely to retain our newfound knowledge, nor is it likely to make
a difference in our lives.

We readily acknowledge that mastering any skill—like piano or
martial arts or surfing—requires a lot of practice. We don't assume that
simply hearing about what to do or being shown how to do it is enough.
We know we will have to practice and experience it for ourselves and
work hard to get better at it. Why do we assume this is not the same for
mental-emotional or consciousness matters?

There are many forces acting on us in our lives that make practicing to change the causes of suffering seem difficult or like an inconvenient distraction. The problem with this disposition is it doesn't take into account the fact that our practice is directly related to our lives and the experiences we are having. There is no "other" life that it is interrupting; it is about the life we are living. Such a practice occurs simply by creating the will to do so and understanding that it will transform the very experiences we call life.

An excerpt from *Whereof One Cannot Speak* speaks to this challenge.

Even if our practice seems genuine and effective, how do we deal with the pain and distractions of life without setting aside the practice? The pull of such forces can seem overwhelming and urgent at times, and any practice can easily be set aside as it is not urgent and is rarely in any way overwhelming. Many people put attention on contemplation when they are either rather bored or feel like it might ease their dissatisfaction with life. I think managing to maintain a practice throughout ups and downs requires understanding that what we're after is the truth, and that never stops being the case no matter what we experience.

We also have to grasp that no matter what we experience, our intent is to discover what's true about that very experience as well as what's true beyond that experience. But even with such a commitment we are still likely to at least temporarily put our practice aside and succumb to pain, self-doubt, and other debilitating reactions from time to time. It's an obstacle that we shouldn't ignore but instead learn to relate to effectively. One way to do that—consistent with a practice committed to discovering the truth—is to investigate the very challenging experience we are enduring and contemplate its nature and why it exists.

LIFE PRACTICES

Discovering the conceptual-activities that create suffering is only the beginning. As you certainly must recognize by now, there is more work to be done. You will need to keep a vigil on this activity and nip it in the bud until your brain learns to stop doing it. Just as important, however, is changing your mental activities to conceptual-actions. Both of these will take practice. You have to be able to instantly recognize when something is a conceptual-activity or conceptual-action and then train yourself to choose action. Again, this takes practice.

The suffering itself, the discord and discomfort, should act as a coach stirring you to take action—now that you know where to look and what to do. So you shouldn't need reminding in order to practice. Unless, of course, you forget it's something you *can* do and fall again into the trap of feeling victim to your own mind. But training yourself is actually up to you.

There are specific exercises, guided meditations, and other practices throughout this book you can use to begin practicing. You also need to glean what areas need attention for you and invent ways to tackle them successfully for yourself. Just remembering to meditate on the mind and experience of a rabbit on a regular basis should help you get a handle on what needs to be done—calming you in the process. Stopping conceptual-activity is one thing, and very important to do, but translating activity into action is also important.

Once you've moved your mind into action, even if this action is conceptual in nature—problem-solving, committing to something, living inside a principle, investigating your experience, contemplating, and so on—you will have transformed your experience and enhanced your life. Because you are still likely to engage in mental activity, such as daydreaming or fantasizing, you need to make sure you recognize it for what it is so that it remains harmless, or better yet, turn it into some form of conceptual-action that produces a result.

Beyond working to end suffering, you've seen there are many practices that fall into the category of conceptual-action that enhance life in some way. You can use contemplation to investigate the source of something experienced in order to get to the bottom of what's going on there. Adopting a principle that demands your mental and physical actions arise consistent with that principle can enhance your self-experience, or your level of skill, and so on. Dwelling on relaxing and calming the mind improves the brain, the nervous system, and alters your state of mind. Practicing changing emotions at will gives a different relationship to and abilities with your emotions. Developing a stronger spatial awareness improves managing your environment. You could take up various practices that increase awareness, improve mind and emotions, heighten sensitivity and health, discover unrecognized aspects of our experience or world, and so on.

There are many other domains of practice that can be taken on to some effect. For example, in one domain a practice could consist of moving your feeling-attention around in the body, in specific ways to increase sensitivity or stimulate the nervous system or help heal some malady. Focusing on feeling parts of the body, like the center, the heart, and so on, produces particular shifts in state that produce consistent results. You can create or learn all kinds of states and feeling-awareness trainings to serve some purpose you have been told or intuit might create beneficial results. (For more on these kinds of practices, see the book *Zen Body-Being*.)

These kinds of practices are usually easier to understand than abstract "spiritual" practices and tend to be less prone to mischief. We like them because they improve our experience of life. Of course, they take work and repetition—pretty much the definition of practice—and so we may be too lazy to take them on. But that is something we can overcome with intent and commitment.

There is no end to the practices we can invent using the mind that could improve our experience and capacities in life. Our main challenge is to keep whatever practice we create or adopt grounded and realistic and not let it become merely abstract or airy-fairy fantasy. But whether grounded or not, we might still find benefit from the attempt, and likely no harm is done no matter what we take on in this way.

Still, you may not believe in many of these kinds of practices. As you know by now, I'm not a fan of beliefs. At best, they are a good guess or a temporary substitute to fill in the gap of seemingly unattainable or inaccessible knowledge. At worst, they are a damaging distortion of what's true. So how do you get around having to believe in these kinds of "mind" practices in order to take them on?

You might notice that weight training builds muscle, so if you want to bulk up you can lift weights and you don't really need to believe or take on faith that this will work. Why? You can observe this in others and also prove it for yourself. Just so, you may not have a firsthand experience with some mental practice, but you can reason it out—especially if you are making it up or even if it's learned from another—that such a training could have beneficial effects and then prove for yourself if this is true or not.

Just like doing physical training to become stronger or more skilled at something, practices using the mind have the same demand of repetition and training. The only thing that would stop you is simply not learning or creating something to practice—the possibilities are endless. Simply choose what kinds of practices to do and where to devote your energy and attention and for what purpose. In relation to ending suffering the only requisite for the practice is that it does just that—and don't forget to frequent your rabbit meditation!

Center Breathing

Let's look a bit into one example of a simple but beneficial practice. The mind and body are inseparably linked. Practices that involve both can have a more inclusive and overall beneficial effect. For example, one simple action people can take to alter their state for the better is to breathe into the center of the body. The center in humans is in the lower abdomen, below the navel and above the pubic bone.

When we breathe, we can do it in basically one of two ways. We can lift the rib cage and so expand the lungs to bring in air. This is most common. We can also lower the diaphragm and pull the lungs down to bring in air. This second action is what I'm referring to.

When you practice breathing down into the very lower part of the abdomen you will focus and stimulate your nervous system in that area. At the same time, you should focus your feeling-attention and mind on this area, as if you are pooling attention on feeling the center of the body. In so doing, in not too much time, your mind will change as will your physiology. This act will tend to calm and quiet the intellectual mind and bring the body to a more present and nonthinking state.

Such breathing can become natural and this is good for the body and mind. If it does become natural it will tend to slip into the background of awareness and probably won't affect your state of mind the same way as doing it on purpose. But even if you train yourself to breathe this way all the time, you can still focus attention and consciously breathe into the center and then it will have the same affect, perhaps even more so because you will be thoroughly grounded in the reality of this shift and can go more deeply into it.

This is a very simple mental and physical practice easily done that can help in many ways. Try it out and see what happens. At first it might take some practice to breathe this way, but once you get into it, you should find out what it can do for you—and just by breathing.

MASTERY AND THE "EFFORTLESS" COMPONENT

Another element that can enhance our work in ending suffering is one of mastery, as we saw with the principles of "Excellence and Mastery." Since life always occurs as process and activity—most of which is repeated—working to develop skill in these undertakings teaches us a great deal about the endeavors we engage and about life in general. When we set the bar at mastery, in at least one or two of our pursuits— and for the rest, simply work on being aware and effective—we invite a deeper level of understanding to emerge. Since we are going to be doing these activities anyway, it makes no sense to do them badly. On the other hand, doing them well not only provides us with greater power and ability, it increases self-esteem and improves our personal self-image.

Pursing mastery, however, demands a great deal of learning. Not just about the activity you're attempting to master but about yourself and your world. It forces you to challenge assumptions and go beyond limitations. In your attempt to master some endeavor you're required to change your perceptions—creating new distinctions and so new experiences you haven't had before—and this provides you with a new understanding and perspective of reality. Sound familiar?

I've found that most people don't think they can actually master anything. But reconsider and imagine that everyone can master something. Maybe they can't master everything or have no desire to master everything, but there is at least one activity in life you can master. Consider how that might contribute to your sense of self and life if you did.

Commensurate with mastery, I've found that committing to the guiding principle of obtaining effortlessness in any practice, art, or activity undertaken provides a great learning tool. Effortlessness doesn't necessarily apply to the efforts involved in the research, investigation, study, and training needed to attain mastery. To be sure, there may well be a lot of effort involved in the search for effortlessness. Effortlessness as a guiding principle, however, demands an unusual and unconventional approach to any matter and so forces us to become conscious of many things that we would not be called on to notice otherwise.

The mere fact of attaining results without effort in domains that are conventionally founded on effort of various kinds throws a monkey wrench into any strategy for how to proceed. Therefore, the first component that enters this pursuit is not-knowing. Because pretty much no one knows how to accomplish effortlessness by doing what they've been doing or applying what they've learned from life thus far, the way to proceed is unknown. This puts the investigation on an unfamiliar footing, requiring an open mind to new possibilities not thought of heretofore. Clearing the slate and creating such openness immediately produces a more genuine and potentially powerful investigation.

The mere fact of pulling ourselves out of the known and putting an open-ended and seemingly incomprehensible task in front of us, draws us to a much deeper and unprecedented level of learning. The search for effortless mastery demands new thinking, experimentation, and unconventional approaches. This in turn demands we stretch beyond our assumptions and beliefs and seek out new principles about how things can work, as well as receive incoming data or feedback without the influence of bias or expectation.

It is rather unimportant whether you achieve mastery or not. The journey itself is transformative. With all of these elements active, you learn a great deal more than most people will ever learn—about yourself, about learning itself, and about life. Certainly, it requires a lot of work and commitment and will dominate your life to a significant extent, but the rewards are great. Life and self are only found within your experience. Shifting your life-commitment to the pursuit of mastery in some area, and perhaps even attaining an experience of mastery, gives you a very different relationship to both self and life than most people enjoy. Since you only have one self and one life, you might want to consider such a path.

UNUSUAL INTERACTIVE PERSPECTIVES

Although I don't tell people how to live their lives, there are guidelines and demands that I do make of those becoming apprentices that I think might be useful for everyone. Here are a few nuggets to consider:

+ Whenever you encounter a problem, get in the habit of seeing it in terms of possible solutions.

- Only protest or complain about something to a person who can do something about it, rather than to those who have no power to change it.
- Keep your word. You don't have to give it, but if you give it, keep it.
- If you misrepresent or say something untrue, clean it up right away—repair any damage you may have caused—and make correction.
- Don't resist making correction when needed; do it as immediately as possible so as not to do more harm by sticking to a mistake or untruth.
- Get more out of whatever you take on than you put into it.
- Don't act out or suppress; communicate instead.

I won't elaborate or explain these. I'll just leave them for you to consider and play with.

NECESSARY SUFFERING?

It might be that no suffering is truly necessary, but when it comes to physical damage or disease this is a different domain than what we have addressed here. Our mental activities may not cause this form of pain but they certainly can contribute much unnecessary distress. Of course, as mentioned, we can indeed affect our physical condition to some degree with our minds, for better or for worse. We can create stress with worry or calm the nervous system with meditation. These clearly have physical effects on the body.

Aside from this influence, let's touch on our relationship to physical pain. I already suggested that we add a lot of discomfort conceptually. To hammer home this point, some time ago an experiment was done with a group of Tibetan monks who'd trained their whole adult lives at controlling their minds and contemplating reality, and another group of regular people who had not. Within this experiment people were subjected to painful electric shock while their brains were being monitored. As I understand it, there was a sound made before the shock, then the shock, and time after the shock, before repeating.

Most people's brains showed increased pain and anxiety before the shock, spiking during the shock, and lingering painful activity after the shock. With the monks on the other hand, there was no activity before the shock, even when they were cued it was coming, there was a spike in the brain during the shock, but afterward there was no distress. We can see in this example, our normal automatic conceptual-activity more than triples the suffering for most people.

What we conceptually add to what's there can dramatically increase and extend the amount of suffering we endure. Alternatively, simply and only experiencing physical pain could be a simple episode that passes quickly. But our conceptual add-ons of fear, anxiety, resistance, resentment, and so on often add most of the discomfort we experience.

You may have heard of me getting my teeth drilled without Novocain, but that is a matter that requires existentially grasping the nature of pain and not producing it. We might consider that is a rather advanced level of conceptual control, but it is still about controlling the mind and not adding what is at its core a concept. I know it is difficult to impossible to consider pain as a concept, and to be clear it is not mere mental activity. What I'm really saying is that pain is a distinction we make; we interpret something as painful by adding this distinction. If we don't do that the experience is not painful.

But this depth of consciousness isn't likely going to be readily available to most people. I'm just saying it actually does work that way, we simply have a hard time seeing it. Certainly, I don't want to give the impression that I go around without pain. Not true. If I stub my toe I'm likely to yell out and hop around in agony for a bit. That comes rather automatically and I don't spend much time and energy fighting the tendency—after all it's just an experience. But the point is that I can, and do sometimes, end pain, and so can you.

But in this consideration, perhaps another story might be more appropriate. I was having acupuncture a long time ago by a traditional Chinese practitioner who plunged the needles unusually deep. I found that although there was some discomfort to the needle, my resistance and anxiety to the next plunge was adding much unnecessary discomfort. When I simply let go and allowed the needle to enter my body without resistance, the discomfort all but disappeared. It really is quite remarkable, and it really does work.

We've seen that worry, for example, adds distress without anything physical occurring. This is all in our minds. With physical pain, strictly speaking, it is not just in our minds, but we also add a great deal. When we stop adding all the conceptual-activity and interpretations that pile on unnecessary pain to even the so-called necessary pain, this experience is far less painful and usually ends sooner.

The point is our resistance to physical pain adds to the pain. Stop resisting and the pain reduces. We might even find that something we thought was physical pain really isn't, or isn't as bad as we thought, once we make this shift. Check it out.

ADDENDUM

A Principle That Could Change Humanity

WHAT IF THERE WAS ONE SIMPLE PRINCIPLE that could transform and empower your ability to live life more effectively, interact with and understand others better, increase your ability to discover and learn, improve your mental sharpness and state of mind, and enliven your perspective? What's more, it's something everyone can do, and if everyone did adopt it the whole planet would improve, conflict would decrease, and growth would be accelerated. Would you be up for adopting such a principle?

This simple principle could be called *questioning*. There can be differing views about what is meant by questioning, so what I'm referring to could be misunderstood. In order for it to work as advertised the actual principle needs to be understood correctly. So let me elaborate and see if I can clarify what I mean.

The kind of questioning I'm talking about begins by acknowledging that we may not know something. This not-knowing isn't a negative malady or a willful ignorance; it doesn't deny what is known or avoid what might be discovered. It simply opens the door to grasping what's true beyond our current level of knowing or consciousness. It is not possible to question or learn or discover anything without not-knowing being available to us. Think about it. How can you learn something if you already know it? That's called knowing, not learning.

So no matter what you know, in order to learn you must step outside of that knowledge. Even if you don't notice it sometimes, whenever you have learned or discovered something, you started with not-knowing because only then can you truly question or investigate or listen. Otherwise, you are simply filling in the blanks with what you already know—or think you know.

We don't want to confuse real questioning for being gullible or prone to fantasy, being open to falling into conspiracy theories, or adopting an ineffective attitude such as "anything is possible," and so on. We want to be grounded and realistic but at the same time open beyond what we think and believe to be true. It might be an open question as to what is possible, but something is true and we need to ground our investigations on seeking what's true and real, not on whimsy or fantasy. Real learning is not about entertaining beliefs or fantasy. We are seeking the truth in whatever way or about whatever subject we may address. This commitment alone changes one's life.

Since much of what we *think* we know comes from hearsay—in other words, from what others have said or asserted—we need to address this form of knowing. Hearsay is not real knowing or experience. In order for it to be real, we need to personally encounter what's true about a subject. How can we assess what's true without having had a personal experience or insight in the matter?

About matters such as philosophies, religions, and whatnot, we don't have to depend on hearsay because we can tackle these subjects directly ourselves and have personal insight. But about domains of knowledge such as scientific information or facts, or why something is the way it is, and the like, it's not practical to investigate everything for ourselves and so we seem dependent to some degree on an outside source.

When it comes to such hearsay, we can start by making a distinction between valid input and mere beliefs or fantasies being proffered. If we use critical thinking and common sense, we can begin by eliminating huge swaths of input as invalid or suspect. As we consider matters with active questioning in mind and are also willing to accept or entertain probabilities that we may not prefer, we can make serious headway in assessing what's "likely" true.

We can also consider the source of the information. Is it considered to be based on fact and does the source have a good track record and is assessed as an honest broker? On the other hand, is the source someone who merely believes something or has a dog in this fight? Just inspecting the source provides us with a way to narrow down what is likely to be factual and what is not. But we have to go further.

Going beyond just trying to sort out hearsay, you can also consider the validity of any belief or knowledge that you have. As you challenge all hearsay, you will notice that most of what you "know" comes from it. Many of your own beliefs will be based on hearsay and the rest will be conclusions you came up with.

When you question what you think and believe, and what you assume and overlook, you are challenging much of what makes up your personal experience. Questioning your own beliefs and even your depth of honesty may be uncomfortable and seem extreme, but if you can't inspect yourself, how can you honestly question anything else? The ability to question yourself, your beliefs, your psychology, your nature, your motives, and so on, is a crucial aspect of the domain of questioning.

I am not suggesting in any way that you depend on your opinions or conclusions as the arbiter of truth. These will always be based on your past, be biased, subjectively limited, and founded on your beliefs and perspective, and so shouldn't be the last word in determining what's true. True questioning doesn't take for granted whatever is believed, or even experienced, as necessarily true or accurate.

I'm also not suggesting that questioning is about being cynical or obstinate. It's more like being willing to learn something new in unexpected places. This creates an openness to wonder what is true beyond our opinions or conclusions and the ability to consider that there could be more that is not perceived or understood.

It is useful to start by questioning your own experience. If you are open to the possibility that you might be wrong about your assessment of something, or about your beliefs or perspectives, you have the power to consider beyond these mental activities—which in essence are really just guesses—and perhaps discover something new or make a correction in your view. You can also investigate such questions as what is mind, how does your brain work, why do you have emotions, is it healthy to judge yourself, and so on. Once you can probe into your own experience, you are better equipped to question and wonder about any other aspect of life or existence.

Questioning shouldn't be thought of as solely, or even mostly, an intellectual exercise. A lot of silence and open focus often accompany it. It involves as much "listening"—to others, yourself, your body, or simply the subject or circumstance—as it does anything else. As well, a feeling-sense component very often accompanies such probing. This feeling-sense is not a reaction or emotion, but more like reaching out with your senses, intuition, patience, and perhaps your "heart and soul" to seek a conscious understanding of something.

An important aspect of this effort is being able to question throughout our experience of life, even in difficult times. What is this experience or feeling about, why does it exist, what is my purpose for having it? This kind of questioning points us into a deeper consciousness as we live life. Living "inside" of circumstantially derived experiences doesn't provide any understanding of what they are and, obviously, provides no freedom from them. Getting "outside" of them, through questioning, does.

Over time this kind of introspection builds and you begin to recognize patterns of mind and are able to cut to the chase much more quickly, and perhaps even bypass some of your more unfruitful tendencies. Some of my abilities to seemingly know about so much is due to encountering so much over time and working it through. In the movie *Groundhog Day*, Bill Murray says to his want-to-be love, "Maybe I'm a god." She challenges him in the negative, and he replies, "But what if a god is just someone who's done life over and over so much that he knows what everything is about?"—or something like that.

I relate to this sentiment. My depth of consciousness isn't a supernatural power so much as a result of questioning for so long and in so many circumstances that eventually a huge amount of breakthroughs, insights, and direct experiences about every nook and cranny of existence has been accumulated. So it may seem like I have an unusual ability or access to a special domain of knowledge, when in fact it is really just the result of a lot of questioning and a lot of hard work. As I've confessed elsewhere, one of my favorite quotes is applicable here:

> *It's not that I'm so much smarter than anyone else,*
> *it's that I stay with the problem longer.*
>
> ALBERT EINSTEIN

This is the only practice you really need.

Deep questioning does not overlook the obvious. For most people one of the more difficult aspects of questioning is to grasp that even the obvious may not be understood as much as it could be. When something seems obvious, we tend to take for granted that we know what it is, how it works, what function it serves, its nature, and so on. Yet when we openly question even the overlooked obvious, looking freshly and without assumption, we can discover some of our most significant insights.

Beyond personal inquiries, an even more profound level of questioning can be accessed by acknowledging foundational and overlooked ignorance. For example, some of the ignored aspects of our experience can be found by noticing that beyond hearsay we personally don't directly know how we came to exist as a self—at one point we became conscious that we exist, but before that we are completely blank—or that we don't know what life really is, or perhaps what consciousness is, or what the intrinsic nature of an object or the absolute nature of existence is, and so on. At this point, we then have a much deeper power to question. This kind of questioning might be called contemplation, and contemplation stands on the possibility that we can personally have direct insights into deep matters beyond hearsay or beliefs.

In order to do this, we have to endow ourselves with the ability to discover whatever is true. For many people this may be a new idea, since we often think that if we haven't personally experienced something first-hand—especially about the more metaphysical, abstract, or spiritual type questions—we can only know what's true from an outside source like science, religion, various belief systems, and so on. But in this way, we can't know for sure. So how do we determine what's true if not from hearsay?

Such an ability would require that we are at the source of obtaining the knowledge we seek. At first blush this may sound like I'm saying that we then draw conclusions or have opinions, but I'm not saying that at all—that would be moving in the wrong direction. For us to directly access an understanding of what's true in some matter, we have to do our own investigations and—depending on what we're talking about—either test and prove our data and insights, or in some cases, become conscious of the real nature of something directly through contemplation.

This second possibility is something we have to prove for ourselves because, like most things, at first it's founded on hearsay. Others claim to have become directly conscious of such matters as one's true nature or the absolute nature of reality—what is sometimes referred to as enlightenment, as in the Zen tradition. But until we access this for ourselves through contemplation and insight we can only intuit that it's possible.

Yet you have to create that it *is* possible or you can't proceed down that road. Most people don't think such direct consciousness is possible. To question at this level, however, that assumption would have to change. When it comes to your own consciousness, self, life, and so on, you are "there" so to speak, you exist *as* and in the middle of these things and so there is no reason you can't become conscious of their true nature.

This possibility generally demands that we focus our attention on a subject, be open to whatever's true no matter what we want, believe, can conceive, or imagine, and intend to grasp its most fundamental nature—beyond beliefs, hearsay, assumptions, preference, or any other biasing factor—until we become directly conscious of what that is. This is a very powerful kind of questioning. But, as we've seen, it is by no means the only possibility within this principle of questioning.

In addition to anything discovered, wondering about whatever we encounter and being curious about things activates a brain activity that leads to growth and clarity. Questioning not only helps keep the brain sharp and slows its deterioration, it provides a physiological and psychological boost that tends to lift your spirits and improve your state of mind. Questioning life or anything in it provides a more open outlook, positive experience, and raises self-esteem because now instead of just being at the effect of circumstance you're examining it, turning it from an imposition to a subject of contemplation.

Once we begin to question life, our experience improves and life becomes an adventure. We not only continuously increase our depth of knowledge and consciousness, we also never run out of subjects to question. We can question any belief or look into what we may be assuming or overlooking. We can contemplate what any aspect of life really is, how it works or came to pass. We can wonder what another's actual experience is and be open to getting their communication. We can ponder and look into what makes us tick, or why our psychology is the way that it is, or why we are feeling whatever we are feeling.

The questions are endless. What is language and how did it come to pass? Why do we obsessively talk to ourselves in our own minds? What is communication, society, life, thought, belief, death? We can question, investigate, or contemplate anything that constitutes life and our experience.

Questioning turns life from merely something to manage into an ongoing adventure, and without changing anything it still makes a huge difference in our experience. Of course, over time we become more and more aware of things we weren't previously, and we might become increasingly conscious of the nature of reality to a depth most never attain. As we progress, we also accumulate a huge reservoir of knowledge. These insights and understandings tend to improve our lives.

It is possible for humanity to understand and adopt this principle. Even if occurring at a very basic level it would still make a huge difference in our reality. Yet as we look at clarifying this task, we see it is likely too complex and detailed for that to happen, but it's worth a try, eh? Even if humanity doesn't adopt the principle of questioning, at least you can. Consider this an invitation to wonder if it's a principle worth adopting.

Index

About the Author

Peter Ralston is one of the founders of the consciousness movement that began in the San Francisco Bay Area—the birthplace for much of the personal growth work generated in the late sixties and early seventies. Although the pursuits were diverse, the overall spirit was one of breaking free from old ways of thinking and creating more powerful ways to live. Peter Ralston was fortunate to study with the top facilitators of this groundbreaking era in human potential; in addition Peter spent thousands of hours in Zen contemplation and participated in dozens of contemplation intensives.

After having several powerful enlightenment experiences in the early seventies, and maturing in his work and teaching, in 1977 Ralston opened his own center in Berkeley, California: the Cheng Hsin School for Ontological Research. Coming directly from the source of the emerging personal growth movement, Ralston's work at the school and his consciousness organization, Empowerment, contributed a powerful new direction, pressing for a deeper level of honesty and a more authentic approach than most other so-called spiritual practices.

He was also the creator of the martial art the Art of Effortless Power. In 1978 he became the first non-Asian to win the full-contact

World Championships held in China. In both his consciousness work and work in physical skill and effective body-being, his approach has always been to lead students away from what is merely believed and toward a powerful personal experience of discovering for themselves what is true.

Ralston has been doing his consciousness work for many decades, facilitating the staff of Lifesprings and Tony Robbins NLP trainings as well as doing workshops for Esalen, Self-Actualizations, Empowerment, and many other organizations around the world. Although many know him for his martial mastery, and as the author of *The Principles of Effortless Power* and *Zen Body-Being*, he is also the creator of a huge body of work known as his Consciousness Work and the author of the powerful trilogy, *The Book of Not Knowing*, *Pursuing Consciousness*, and *The Genius of Being*.

His website is **PeterRalston.com**.